Indian Gold Coins

of the

⤙ 20TH CENTURY ⤚

by

Mike Fuljenz

A special thank you to my wife Karen, my son Jake and my daughter Katie

Sincere thanks to Gary Alexander, Dwayne Basset, Rick Busby, William C., Trey Cox, Beth Deisher, Kenny Duncan, David Hall, Forest Hamilton, Terry Hanlon, Stacey Hebert, Vickie Hernandez, Brian Hodge, Jerry Jordan, Ray Knight, Brian Mack, Robert McGee, Todd McKinley, Michael Miers, Lee Minshull, Jill Mitchell, Rick Montgomery, Paul Montgomery, Robert Patton, Amy Powell, Sid Reichenberger, Ed Reiter, Lee Sanders, Scott Schechter, Miles Standish, Paul Stein, Scott Travers, Arnold U., Ryan Verde, Matt Willey, Doug Winter, as well as the countless others who have given their time and talent throughout the creation of this book.

Also, many thanks to all the collectors I've worked with over the years.

Copyright © 2010 by Mike Fuljenz

Published by Subterfuge Publishing
PO Box 8008
Lumberton, Texas 77657
www.subterfugepublishing.com

ISBN - 10: 0981948898
ISBN - 13: 9780981948898

Library of Congress Control Number: 2010926947

Printed in the United States of America

www.mikefuljenz.com

TABLE OF CONTENTS

When it comes to baseball, Mike Fuljenz roots for the Astros. But when it comes to coins, he's a huge fan of the Indians – especially those whose likenesses appear on U.S. gold coins.

Mike has now written a new book on these Indians – and in it, he pulls off a rare triple play.

The book is called Indian Gold Coins of the 20th Century, and it contains a date-by-date analysis of all three gold coins issued by the U.S. Mint during the 1900s whose designs portray American Indians.

Mike wrote about two of these coins – the Indian Head eagle ($10 gold piece) and quarter eagle ($2.50 gold piece) in two previous books. Now he has updated the contents of those two books and combined them in a single volume, along with totally new text on the third 20th-century coin in this trifecta, the Indian Head half eagle ($5 gold piece).

The result is the numismatic equivalent of a grand slam home run.

After decades as a professional numismatist, Mike Fuljenz is a leading expert on U.S. gold coinage – and coins that portray American Indians have always been among his personal favorites.

This is reflected in Mike's new book. Like his previous ones, it's a treasure trove of fascinating facts and priceless pointers.

The three gold coins featured in the book were made by the Mint from 1907 to 1933 – a period that took the nation from the death of horse-drawn carriages to the depths of the Great Depression.

The two-and-a-half tumultuous decades between those historic bookends witnessed some of the century's most memorable events. The opening of the Panama Canal … the horrors of World War I … the dawn of automobiles and aviation … the start of the federal income tax … the coming of women's suffrage … the gangster-ridden age of Prohibition … the onset of radio, sound recordings and Hollywood "talkies" – all of this was taking place in the years when these three coins were part of American commerce.

Indian Head gold coins didn't spend much time in most Americans' pockets. Five dollars represented more than a day's pay for many at the time, so gold coins of any kind saw very little use in everyday transactions at the local A&P or the 5-and-10-cent store.

The fact is, Indian Head half eagles weren't even issued in 12 of the 22 years they were nominally part of the coinage lineup. After being minted annually from 1908 through 1916, they weren't produced again until 1929 – the very last year of their all-too-brief existence. There are only 24 date-and-mint combinations in the series.

The quarter eagles were minted in only 13 years between 1908 and 1929, the eagles in just 15 between 1907 and 1933.

But, while their life spans weren't long, all three coins are rich in historical interest – and their stories are especially compelling at a time when gold itself is stirring so much excitement in the marketplace. Reading the new book is a great way to study this legacy and to learn the fine points that make certain dates – and certain coins – scarcer and more valuable than others.

All three coins came into being largely through the efforts of President Theodore Roosevelt. "TR" was a hands-on president with wide-ranging interest in many different facets of American life and culture, and his "pet crime," as he called it, was to upgrade the aesthetics of U.S. coinage in the glorious tradition of ancient Greece.

Roosevelt personally recruited Augustus Saint-Gaudens, the pre-eminent American sculptor of the day, to play a major part in this process, and Saint-Gaudens created two magnificent coins – a $20 gold piece depicting Miss Liberty in full stride and a $10 gold piece featuring the likeness of a classical Lady Liberty adorned with a ceremonial Indian headdress.

The $10 gold piece is the Indian Head eagle showcased by Mike Fuljenz in his books. It was Roosevelt's idea to mix the jarringly unrelated symbols of a Grecian goddess and Indian regalia – and in Saint-Gaudens' gifted hands, the combination not only seems plausible but has an elegant look.

Saint-Gaudens died in 1907, shortly before the release of his beautiful coins, and Roosevelt faced the daunting task of finding a replacement to redesign the two remaining gold coins, the half eagle and quarter eagle. He was aided by a close friend, prominent Boston physician William Sturgis Bigelow, who gave him both a plan and an artist to carry it out.

Bigelow collected fine art, and he was intrigued by the use of incuse relief in ancient Egyptian artworks. Incusing is a technique in which design elements are recessed below the surface, rather than raised above it. There was no modern precedent for using such relief in minting coins, but Bigelow talked Roosevelt into giving it a try on the two smallest U.S. gold coins, whose Coronet design had been basically unchanged for nearly 70 years.

The man he recommended, Boston sculptor Bela Lyon Pratt, was two decades younger and far less renowned than the great Saint-Gaudens had been, but his work was impressive – and though he was only 40, he already enjoyed wide recognition in the art world.

Following Bigelow's guidelines, which Roosevelt had approved, Pratt came up with artwork in which the design elements are recessed below a plane that is uniformly flat. In short, he used incuse – or "sunken" – relief. The obverse depicts an Indian brave wearing a traditional war bonnet, while the reverse shows an eagle in repose, perched upon fasces and an olive branch – symbols of preparedness and peace.

Whereas Saint-Gaudens had fashioned separate designs for the eagle and double eagle, Pratt's two coins both carry the same design, differing in just their size and statement of value.

Although they're not as dazzling as the two Saint-Gaudens coins, the Pratt gold coins possess a degree of innovation that may very well exceed that of any other U.S. coins – including the master's far more acclaimed creations. To this day, they remain the only U.S. coins whose designs are entirely incuse. Nor are they short on aesthetic appeal.

Unlike the mixed metaphor on Saint-Gaudens' $10 gold piece, the Indian brave portrayed by Pratt is true-to-life in a powerful, dignified way. Indeed, it compares favorably with the composite portrait of actual Indian chiefs on the buffalo nickel, a far more fondly remembered coin that came along five years later. Pratt's eagle is remarkably similar to the one on Saint-Gaudens' $10 gold piece, even to the point of having a similar perch. It complements the Indian portrait perfectly.

The incusing that makes Pratt's coins so unique helps explain why his artistry is under-appreciated: The device serves to mask the subtlety and strength of the designs. The Indian portrait doesn't stand out artistically, as it were, partly because it doesn't stand out – quite literally – on the coins themselves.

The Indian Head half eagle and quarter eagle pose special challenges for graders – again because their features are sunken below the surface, not raised above it like those on standard U.S. coins. That's a major reason why Mike Fuljenz' new book is such a great gift for those who collect these series.

Mike's date-by-date analysis is a road map to the most significant factors in determining the grade of every coin in every series – including not only focal points common to all date-and-mint varieties but also characteristics found only on certain coins. These expert insights can make an enormous difference in judging the grade – and therefore the value – of any particular Indian Head gold coin, and that can be much more than just a gift of knowledge. For some it can be the key to substantial monetary gain.

Mike's trilogy of books on Indian Head gold coins underscores how often American Indian themes have appeared on U.S. coinage – even during times when Indian tribes were engaged in open, bloody conflict with the government.

The first U.S. coins to portray American Indians were the 1854 gold dollar and $3 gold piece. From then until 1889, Indian Head portraits were featured on two different types of gold dollars (the "Small Head" and "Large Head" versions), and the $3 gold piece carried what collectors call the "Indian Princess Head."

The Indian Head cent became the first widely used coin with an Indian motif when it was introduced in 1859. It remained in production until 1909 – by which time the conflicts with Indian tribes had ended and Indians were perceived more sympathetically as symbols of an earlier, far more rugged time in American history. Interestingly, however, the "Indian" on the cent was actually a Caucasian wearing an Indian headdress.

The buffalo nickel, also sometimes known as the Indian Head nickel, is surely the best-known – and best-loved – U.S. coin to bear an Indian's likeness. Nonetheless, most people associate this coin with the animal rather than the Indian. Admittedly, the American bison shown on the nickel's reverse complements the obverse perfectly, since this massive, shaggy animal was the primary source of sustenance for Indian tribes living on the Great Plains prior to white settlers' arrival in the mid- and late 19th century.

This is among many instances where the same coin can be known by different names. Even the Indian Head half eagle and quarter eagle are sometimes referred to as the Pratt gold coins, in honor of their designer.

Mike Fuljenz explored this interesting subject in a highly entertaining and instructive article in the January 2010 issue of the monthly magazine COINage – and that article is reprinted, with minor modifications. Mike also expertly instructs on how to best sell your gold coins quickly and how to best protect them from theft in this handy book.

After the buffalo nickel, no further Indian themes would grace regular U.S. coinage until the year 2000. But they did appear quite frequently on U.S. commemorative coins during that program's "traditional" period, from 1892 to 1954.

Among the commemoratives that depicted American Indians were half dollars honoring the Arkansas Centennial, Daniel Boone Bicentennial, Long Island Tercentenary, Missouri Centennial, Oregon Trail Memorial and Providence Tercentenary.

In 2000, the Mint began striking base-metal circulating $1 coins bearing the likeness of Sacagawea, a Shoshone Indian woman who served the Lewis and Clark Expedition as a translator and guide. The coin remains in production today, and in 2009, the Mint began using its reverse to showcase a variety of Indian-related themes.

In 2001, the Mint revived and modified the buffalo nickel design for use on a commemorative silver dollar. This "American Buffalo" coin proved so popular with collectors that orders exceeded its mintage limit of 500,000 pieces almost immediately.

In 2006, production began on a one-ounce gold bullion coin likewise bearing a very close facsimile of the buffalo nickel's design, and this .9999-fine coin – also called the American Buffalo – got a similarly enthusiastic welcome from collectors and investors. It's now a regular part of the Mint's annual line of bullion products.

Mike Fuljenz doesn't cover all these other coins in his new book. But they demonstrate how closely American Indians' heritage is intertwined with that of the nation itself.

His books shine a spotlight on that relationship. In the process, he gives his readers a greater appreciation for why these themes were chosen in the first place. *Indian Gold Coins of the 20th Century* is a scorecard no collectors should be without if they want to tell the "players" in these three exciting lineups of U.S. coins. With the help of this endlessly fascinating book, they're sure to be winners every time.

A HISTORY OF THE INDIAN HEAD QUARTER & HALF EAGLES

Conceived in controversy, born of conflict, and reviled at birth, the $2.50 and $5 Indian Head Quarter Eagles overcame there rocky beginnings to become two of America's most popular gold coins. The tale of these extraordinary coins ripple with the sinews of high drama and political intrigue, of powerful ambition hammering against bureaucratic inertia, of soaring imagination transcending drab intellect.

This is the story of two coins, yes, but it is also the story of a nation growing up, a young country coming of age and proclaiming its unique character as it demands a place of respect on the world stage. The Indian Head Quarter Eagle and its big brother, the Indian Head Half Eagle, manifested a visionary president's declaration to the global community that America was not just a rebellious offspring of the Old World but a fresh idea in its own right to be taken quite seriously indeed.

A NUMISMATIC REVOLUTION TAKES SHAPE

John Singer Sargent's 1903 portrait of Theodore Roosevelt (now hangs in the White House)

In 1901, a crazed anarchist assassin's bullets felled President William McKinley and thrust a feisty youthful Teddy Roosevelt into the White House. Not yet 43, Roosevelt became America's youngest president.

He attacked the challenges of the presidency with the vigorous gusto he had demonstrated in leading the charge of the Rough Rider Regiment up San Juan Hill in the Spanish-American War. Roosevelt saw much in the nation that needed fixing and set his boundless energy and bulldog determination to the task. "I always believe in going hard at everything," he often said.

One target of his sweeping reform campaign was American coinage, which stagnated with designs that were boring and uninspired when they were new and had not grown more endearing with age. The penny

≈ 1 ≈

had carried the same tired design for over forty years. The $20 Gold Double Eagle had looked the same to three generations of Americans. The Eagle, Half Eagle and Quarter Eagle carried the same countenance for nearly seven decades.

Grumbling about the coin designs began bubbling up as early as 1879, according to numismatic historian Dr. Thomas Fitzgerald. "The criticisms continued and grew louder following the striking of the 'Bland' silver dollar (Morgan), the Barber nickel and silver coins along with the unchanged gold designs dating back over sixty years. The Treasury Department considered a contest to redesign the coinage: even a public competition with Augustus Saint-Gaudens, Henry Mitchell and Charles Barber acting as judges in 1891. The results were poor and Saint-Gaudens reportedly told Mint Director Frank Leach that there were only four competent coin designers known, of which three were in France and Saint-Gaudens was the fourth."

Roosevelt bristled at the "stupefying mediocrity" (Breen 1988) of United States coin design, which he described as an abomination "artistically of atrocious hideousness." The man who built the Panama Canal and enforced the Monroe Doctrine with gunboat diplomacy demanded respect for his nation as he put the world on notice it had better not mess with America. He believed that a nation's coinage was its sovereign signature, and he was convinced it should be signed with a bold stroke that commanded respect and left no doubt about the forceful personality of America at the dawn of the 20th century.

Roosevelt made no secret of his contempt for the colorless drudges at the U.S. Mint headed by chief engraver Charles E. Barber. Barber's designs exhibited all the excitement of a cold, soggy bowl of oatmeal. Roosevelt concluded that the creative well at the Mint was dry, and he would have to take unconventional measures to whip up the creative energy needed to fulfill his vision.

Winning a mandate to the presidency on his own merit in the 1904 election, Roosevelt was emboldened to commit what he called his "pet crime" of transforming United States coinage to a state of pride and respect…even if it meant trampling roughshod over the established inbred Washington political cliques.

What he accomplished revolutionized American coinage. Over the next fourteen years, every U.S. coin denomination would be revitalized with some of the most stunning designs in American numismatic history – before or since.

Believing it hopeless to expect anything more than the mundane from the bureaucratic hacks at the Mint, Roosevelt looked outside the usual channels for inspiration. He had been much impressed by the work of famed Boston sculptor Augustus Saint-Gaudens with whom he had struck up a close friendship. Saint-Gaudens designed Roosevelt's 1905 inaugural medal.

On a cold November night in 1905, the two friends fell into a discussion about U.S. coinage. They agreed that radical changes were needed. Both men admired the drama and visual impact of ancient high-relief coinage and the Renaissance medals of Pisanello and Sperandio. The discussion grew more animated as the vision took form in their minds. Saint-Gaudens' son Homer later detailed how "they both grew enthusiastic over the old high-relief Greek coins" as each fed on the creative energy of the other until at last "the President declared that he would have the mint stamp a modern version of such coins in spite of itself if my father would design them…the Cent, the Eagle, and the Double Eagle."

Saint-Gaudens eagerly accepted the challenge, even though he knew he would have to hurry. He had learned five years earlier that he was dying of cancer. Though he continued to work, his health was fading rapidly. Time was short. The 20th century American numismatic revolution was put into motion.

A RADICAL DESIGN CONCEPT

The opening volley of the revolution achieved a monumental creative victory greater than even the ambitious Teddy Roosevelt had hoped for. Despite dogged interference and attempts at sabotage by an obstinate and embittered Charles Barber, the collaboration of Roosevelt and Saint-Gaudens produced the exquisite Eagle and spectacular Double Eagle coin that bears Saint-Gaudens' name.

The Double Eagle he created is often described as the most beautiful coin in American history. So timeless was the design that the obverse is still used today on American Eagle coins, nearly a century after its debut.

Sadly, Augustus Saint-Gaudens died before he could see the revolution to conclusion. In fact, he didn't even live to see his beautiful coin creations put into production. But his death in 1907 did not stop the movement. One of his students was called to duty to take up the banner and complete his mission.

Elated by the artistic success of the Double Eagle and Eagle, Roosevelt immediately turned his attention to the other gold coin denominations. Another close friend of President Roosevelt came forward with a novel and radical proposal for the design of the Half Eagles and Quarter Eagles.

Dr. William S. Bigelow, a prominent Boston physician, was actively involved with the Boston Museum of Fine Arts, where he had seen and been intrigued by the incuse style of ancient Egyptian artwork. Numismatic expert Walter Breen described how these artworks inspired a coin design:

Dr. William Sturgis Bigelow

> "Around New Year's Day, 1908, Dr. William Sturgis Bigelow, an intimate friend of Pres. Theodore Roosevelt, got the idea of making coins with devices sunk beneath the fields - not true intaglio, but rather with relief designs depressed so that the highest points would not be at once worn away, somewhat in the manner of certain Egyptian Fourth Dynasty stelae."

Bigelow reasoned that this technique of depressing the image below the coin surface would eliminate the problems encountered with Saint-Gaudens' high-relief designs for the Double Eagle, which exposed the raised parts to excessive wear and made stacking the coins difficult.

Though the incuse technique was considered a radical new coin design concept in the early 20th century, Bigelow was not the first to propose it for an American coin. More than a hundred years earlier, in 1792 a Philadelphia publisher named Matthew Carey suggested intaglio coins with a recessed design to prevent wear on the design. His proposal was not implemented and was soon forgotten.

The concept of incuse coins originated in ancient times. Frank Leach, who presided as Mint Director during Roosevelt's overhaul of the nation's coinage, wrote in his "Recollections of a Newspaper Man, " "Confirming the truth of the old saying, 'there is nothing new in the world,' we found, in looking over some authorities on ancient coinage, that almost the very first attempt making coins was by depressing or incusing the designs."

Bigelow suggested the incuse technique to the President. Roosevelt, ever the innovator, liked the idea greatly even though, according to Frank Leach, it was a departure from the original plan for the coins:

"Originally it was the intention to give the $5 and $2.50 pieces the same design as that used on the Double Eagle or $20 piece, but before final action to that end was taken President Roosevelt invited me to lunch with him at the White House. His purpose was to have me meet Doctor William Sturgis Bigelow of Boston, a lover of art and friend of the President, who was showing great interest in the undertaking for improving the appearance of American coins, and who had a new design for the smaller gold coins. It was his idea that the commercial needs of the country required coins that would "stack" evenly, and that the preservation of as much as possible of the flat plane of the piece was desirable."

Roosevelt gave Bigelow the green light to pursue getting the revolutionary designs done for the Quarter and Half Eagle gold coins. Leach had no choice but to go along with the president's decision.

INCUSE OR NOT?

According to numismatic scholar Dr. Thomas Fitzgerald, the term "incuse" is commonly, and mistakenly, used to describe the technique Bigelow recommended for the gold coins. However, a true incuse image would be a fully negative image impressed into the metal in what is sometimes called "hollow relief." The actual technique used by Pratt was in fact a positive image recessed into the metal so its raised features were below the surface plane of the coin.

Numismatic writers sometimes refer to the Pratt design as "incused relief," which seems like a contradiction in terms but is technically closer to being accurate than simply "incuse." Pratt's Indian Head is a relief image incused at its edges into the surface of the coin.

Though "incuse" is imprecise in describing the Pratt design, "for most collectors the difference is irrelevant," says Douglas Mudd, Curator of Exhibitions at the American Numismatic Association. Persistent and pervasive misuse over time has legitimized the term for common usage.

Nonetheless, it's an interesting bit of coin trivia to stir conversation at coin club meetings.

VICTORY OVER BUREAUCRACY

With the president's blessing and over the Mint's objections, Bigelow set about securing exactly the right talent to execute his idea. Through their mutual interest in the Boston Museum of Fine Arts, Bigelow knew and admired Boston sculptor Bela Lyon Pratt, who had been a student of Augustus Saint-Gaudens. Bigelow approached Pratt about the assignment and persuaded the respected artist to accept the challenge.

Pratt plunged into the assignment with zest. For the reverse, he adapted the Standing Eagle from Saint-Gaudens' ten-dollar coin, a tribute to his former mentor. It may also have been a sly jab in the ribs of mint engraver Charles Barber, whose notion of the ideal eagle was the awkward Great Seal eagle that plagued the quarter and half dollar of the time – a Barber design. Walter Breen supposed that Pratt's eagle, as designed, "must have been worthy of a J.J. Audubon." That was before Charles Barber got his hamfisted hands on it.

"Pratt, Bela Lyon" filled the obverse with the face of an aging Indian warrior in full headdress to represent an "impression emblematic of Liberty" as required by the Mint Act of 1792. The striking image set a milestone for American coin design. In his prize-winning essay "Glory Years: The Numismatic Revolution of 1907-1921, the Men Behind It, and Their Designs," Brian Rose noted, "This design marked the beginning of a new age in numismatics: the age of photographic naturalism, and pointed out the way for the work of Victor Brenner [Lincoln penny] and James Earle Fraser [Buffalo/Indian Head nickel]."

Pratt delivered his designs by mid-1908. President Roosevelt liked them. Bigelow beamed with pride. Roosevelt ordered the models dispatched forthwith to the Mint for immediate production of master dies, hubs, and working dies. He wanted the public to see the new coins as soon as possible.

But Charles Barber, the consummate bureaucratic foot-dragger, defied the president — from stubbornness, stupidity, or both — and held up production for months. He fiddled with Pratt's designs, complaining of this supposed flaw and that, making unneeded changes, and procrastinating in the apparent hope he could make the designs go away by neglect. He clearly did not comprehend that he was dealing with a president to whom "no" was not an acceptable answer.

In the end, Barber's obstructionist tactics failed to kill the project. Although he did managed to dilute the visual impact of Pratt's creations somewhat, it is a testament to the power of Pratt's artistic genius that even Barber's chronic mediocrity could not completely camouflage the brilliance of the designs.

The dies were finally finished and delivered to the Coiner's Department to begin production.

A FIRESTORM OF CONTROVERSY

The first Indian Head Quarter Eagles left the Mint on October 9, 1908 and at last went into circulation in November. It had taken nearly a year from the time Dr. Bigelow conceived the design concept to get the finished coins into the public's hands.

President Roosevelt sent a letter to Pratt thanking him for the "great service you have rendered the country."

The arrival of the radical new coin design on the public scene met with mixed reaction. There were those who admired the artistic beauty of the design. Others raised a great cry of criticism.

Pratt's design had champions other than his patrons Bigelow and Roosevelt. Writer Chandler Post praised Pratt for his naturalistic depiction of a true native Indian, a feat which Post maintained was rarely achieved in sculpting.

However, there were plenty of critics to disagree…quite vocally. Though some of the complaints held merit, much of the adverse re-action was simply to something new and non-traditional.

A 1908 issue of The Numismatist called the Pratt design for the Quarter and Half Eagles a "novelty in modern coinage, but one that for various reasons has been adversely commented upon by both artist, banker and citizen when opinions have been solicited."

The loudest voice among the detractors – at least the one who gets the most ink in historical references – was longtime Philadelphia numismatist S.H. Chapman. Chapman was so incensed by the Pratt Quarter Eagle that in December 1908 he fired off a steaming hot letter to President Roosevelt lambasting the coin as being ugly, easily counterfeited, and unhygienic:

"It was the hope of every one that when our new coinage appeared we would have one of great beauty and artistic merit. But the new $5 and $2.50 gold pieces just issued totally lack these qualities, and not only those of beauty, but actually miss the practicability to which every effect of beauty in relief has been sacrificed.

The idea of Dr. Bigelow to sink the whole relief below the flat surface of the coin causes it to appear like a design merely incised in the blank, and precludes entirely the effect of miniature bas-relief.

The head of the Indian is without artistic merit, and portrays an Indian who is emaciated, totally unlike the big, strong Indian chiefs as seen in real life.

The treatment of the head is crude and hard, with sharp, abrupt outlines as if carved by a mere metal chaser; and on the reverse is a reproduction of the Saint-Gaudens' eagle, which represents not our national bird [the bald eagle] but resembles more closely the golden eagle, which is also indigenous to Europe.

The placing of the design below the surface of the flan, with deeply incised outlines, gives the effect of having been engraved into the metal, and can, therefore, be closely imitated by any metal chaser with the graver, without dies or moulds. And I am certain that if this had been suggested to the secret service officials it would never have been issued by the Treasury Department, and the issuance ought to be immediately stopped and the coins recalled, for every one will be in danger of the imitations.

The sunken design, especially the deeply sunken portion of the neck of the Indian, will be a great receptacle for dirt and conveyor of disease, and the coin will be the most unhygienic ever issued."

Chapman also objected to what he considered to be poor stacking qualities of the coin. Because it was thinner than its predecessor, Chapman pointed out, the coin stacks made by banks would not be of uniform size, especially when mixed with the older coins.

Chapman could find nothing good to say about the new Quarter Eagle and demanded nothing less than that they be erased in total:

> "These coins will be a disgrace to our country as a monument of our present ideas of art as applied to coinage. As compared with those of recent issues of European countries, not to mention the beautiful works of the ancient Greek coin engravers, it is an utterly miserable, hideous production, and let us hope that its issue will not be continued and that it will be recalled and remelted."

Roosevelt forwarded Chapman's letter to Dr. Bigelow. Why to Bigelow and not to Pratt? Roosevelt apparently looked upon Bigelow as a project manager of sorts with responsibility for the coin.

Bigelow shot back a sharply-worded rebuttal three days later:

> "He [Mr. Chapman] says 'sinking the relief below the surface makes it look like an incised design and precludes the effect of a bas-relief. This is hardly correct, as Mr. Chapman can readily see for himself in photographs of the Egyptian sculptures. The bas-relief effect is accentuated and not diminished by the shadow of the sharp outline.
>
> He says the head of the Indian is 'without artistic merit and portrays and Indian who is emaciated, totally unlike the big, strong Indian chiefs as seen in real life.' The answer to this is that the head was taken from a recent photograph of an Indian whose health was excellent. Perhaps Mr. Chapman has in mind the fatter but less characteristic type of Indian sometimes seen on the reservations.
>
> [Regarding the eagle's authenticity] …an absolutely correct representation of the white-headed American eagle.

[Regarding ease of counterfeiting] This criticism can hardly be taken seriously. If a forger were going to engrave anything, he would not waste his labor on a single coin. It would be as easy to engrave a die [thereby allowing him to make hundreds or thousands of coins.]

[Regarding the unhygienic qualities] This remains to be seen. The question of hygiene has more relation to silver coins than gold, as they find their way into dirtier pockets. A dirty gold coin would be an anomaly. I have never happened to see one.

[Regarding stacking and thickness] What Mr. Chapman says in regard to this is perfectly true. I noticed it as soon as they were issued and called Mr. Leach's attention to it. It proved to be due to an accidental warping of the steel die in hardening. Mr. Leach tells me that it can and will be avoided in the future. I agree with Mr. Chapman that it would be well if all the coins in circulation were of the same thickness."

Chapman was not mollified by Bigelow's response and again wrote to the President offering a point by point rebuttal of Bigelow's arguments. The letter included another jab at the health of the Indian shown on the coin and pointing out that in California there were plenty of filthy gold coins. His vigorous opposition failed to move the President, however, and the Bigelow-Pratt Quarter Eagle remained in circulation.

The general public took the new coin design mostly in stride. The average American could not usually afford to carry gold coins as pocket change. While gold coins still circulated in some parts of the West, in the more populous East they were mostly stacked in bank vaults.

SHORT LIFE FOR THE LAST QUARTER EAGLE

The "2½ Indian," as it has become known among coin collectors, had a relatively short life as American coin designs go. It was minted from 1908 to 1929, but not continuously. Production was stopped after 1915. Production was suspended for an eight-year gap from 1916 to 1924. Many were melted in 1916 as unsold.

The Philadelphia Mint furnished most of the Indian Head Quarter Eagles, with sporadic assists from the Denver Mint in 1911, 1914, and 1925. Just 15 coins make up the entire set — 12 from the Philadelphia Mint and three from Denver.

Since there was little call for them in day-to-day commerce, production usually cranked up toward the end of the year to meet demand for Christmas gifts. By late January, most of them had found their way back into the various subtreasury vaults.

Production of the Indian Head Quarter Eagle resumed in 1925 but the economic collapse beginning in 1929 made the coin no longer useful. Not only was production of the 2½ Indian Head Quarter Eagle halted for good, but it marked the end of the $2.50 coin denomination in American coinage. The Indian Head was the last American Quarter Eagle.

THE LAST CIRCULATING HALF EAGLE

The fact is, Indian Head Half Eagles weren't even issued in 12 of the 22 years they were nominally part of the coinage lineup. After being minted annually from 1908 through 1916, they weren't produced again until 1929 – the very last year of their all-too-brief existence. There are only 24 date and mint combinations in the series.

The $5 Indian, unlike the $2 ½ Indian was struck in San Francisco and New Orleans. The establishment of The Federal Reserve in 1913 played a part in the public opting for paper money over gold coins for routine daily transactions.

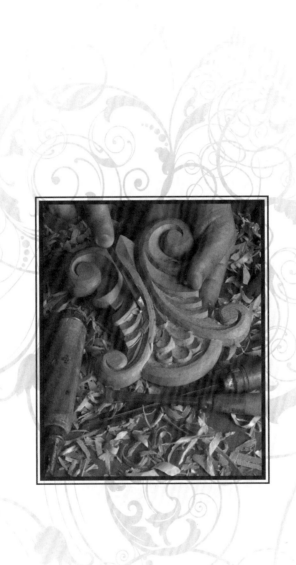

DESIGN DETAILS OF THE INDIAN HEAD QUARTER & HALF EAGLES

Teddy Roosevelt launched an artistic renaissance in American coin design that swept across all denominations. Coin historians call it The Golden Age of American coinage.

It began with a conversation in November 1905 between Roosevelt and sculptor Augustus Saint-Gaudens. "I want to make a suggestion," Roosevelt told the famed artist in November 1905. "It seems to be worthwhile to try for a really good coinage, though I suppose there will be a revolt about it!"

Roosevelt laid out his grand plan to reshape the look of American coinage and entreated the sculptor to be his co-conspirator against the deadheads at the U.S. Mint. He mused, only partly in jest, that their plot would "seriously increase the mortality among the employees of the Mint," concluding that they would "perish in a good cause."

The revolution began with the spectacular Saint-Gaudens Eagle and Double Eagle designs and continued through the Bigelow-Pratt Quarter and Half Eagle, then on to Victor D. Brenner's Lincoln penny and James Earle Fraser's Buffalo/Indian Head nickel. The silver coins soon followed with Adolph A. Weinman's famed Mercury dime and Walking Liberty half dollar along with Hermon A. MacNeil's classic Standing Liberty quarter and Anthony De Francisci's Peace Dollar.

By 1921, the revolution was won, and the Golden Age of America's coinage produced some of the most aesthetically pleasing coins in the world.

THE GOLDEN AGE OF AMERICAN COINAGE

Lincoln Penny

Mercury Dime

Indian Head Quarter Eagle

Buffalo Nickel

Standing Liberty Quarter

Indian Head Eagle

Walking Liberty Half Dollar

Peace Dollar

Saint-Gaudens Double Eagle

UNCHARTED DESIGN TERRITORY

In several respects, Bela Lyon Pratt's design for the Quarter and Half Eagle gold coins was the most revolutionary and innovative of all the "radical" Golden Age coins. It was the first American coin to use the incused relief technique, the first American coin to depict a realistic Indian image, and among the first American coins to be produced in matte proofs (not Pratt's idea).

The obverse of Pratt's Quarter Eagle depicts an authentic-looking Indian chief in a war bonnet, with the date, 13 stars (six left, seven right), and the motto LIBERTY forming a circle around him. Pratt inscribed his initials "BLP" above the date.

The reverse shows an eagle in repose, perched upon fasces and an olive branch. The fasces (a bundle of rods containing an ax with a projecting blade, carried in front of magistrates in ancient Rome) symbolizes preparedness, the olive branch peace. Pratt managed to work in four different inscriptions on the reverse without making the design appear cluttered or unbalanced. The reverse bears the words:

UNITED STATES OF AMERICA • E PLURIBUS UNUM

IN GOD WE TRUST • 2½ DOLLARS

Brian Rose, in his essay "The Numismatic Revolution of 1907-1921, the Men Behind It, and Their Designs," credits Pratt and Bigelow with launching a new age of numismatic design, the age of photographic realism.

> "In contrast with the strong Greek influences upon the Saint-Gaudens coins, Pratt and Bigelow based the new Half and Quarter-Eagles primarily on Middle Eastern and Egyptian art; in fact, Bigelow first struck upon the idea of an incused coin while viewing the Boston Museum of Fine Art's collection of Egyptian reliefs. Pratt's incused designs for the Eagle and Quarter-Eagle represented the transition from classical art to modern. For the reverse, he used a nearly identical version of the Standing Eagle Saint-Gaudens used for the ten-dollar coin-a tribute to the late sculptor and to classic Greek art. For the obverse, he created an aged Indian warrior in full headdress, surrounded by thirteen stars. This design marked the beginning of a new age in numismatics: the age of photographic naturalism, and pointed out the way for the work of Victor Brenner and James Earl Fraser."

Critic's exceptions notwithstanding, Pratt's depiction of an American Indian represented a dramatic change in the way the American native was portrayed on American coinage. Pratt was the first to show a true Indian profile with a genuine headdress on a coin.

CHANGING STYLE OF AMERICAN INDIAN MOTIFS

Previous Indian motifs on U.S. coins had been stylistic fantasies, even including the much-admired Saint-Gaudens $10 Indian gold piece. Designers typically portrayed the classic profile of Lady Liberty topped off with a feathered bonnet reminiscent of cigar store wooden Indians which bore no resemblance to any authentic headdress actually worn by a real native chieftain.

Essayist Steven Roach characterized how depictions of the American Indian varied according to the times:

> "It has been said that American art of the late nineteenth century seems to owe more to theatrics than to observation. As the twentieth century emerged, the Indian became a vanishing

Massachusetts 1787 half cent believed to be the first coin in America to portray an Indian image

species and the artist's depiction of the West changed to represent it as it had been, and to memorialize the American Indian. Changes in the depiction of the American Indian have been as varied as the Indians themselves, but it has not of itself been any guarantee of quality art. At best, the pieces are expressive, emotional, and personal, but at worst, the Indian has merely been a form of genre which is stereotyped, overblown, and repetitive."

The Massachusetts 1787 copper half cent was probably the first coin in North America to depict an Indian, standing with a bow in one hand and an arrow in the other. Variations on the same design appeared at intervals in post-colonial coinage.

On regular issue U.S. coins, the Indian motif didn't appear until the mid-19th century with the introduction of James B. Longacre's Indian Princess Head dollar and three dollar gold pieces. Longacre modified the theme with a different headdress for the 1859 Indian Head cent. Saint-Gaudens' 1907 Indian Head Eagle continued the convention of depicting a classical Greco-Roman profile of Lady Liberty topped with a fanciful head covering intended to look like an Indian headdress.

PROGRESSION OF INDIAN IMAGES ON REGULAR ISSUE U.S. COINS

*1854 Indian
Princess $3*

*1854 Indian
Princess Head $1*

*1859 Indian
Head Cent*

*1907 Indian
Head Eagle*

*1929 Indian Head
Quarter Eagle*

*1913 Buffalo/Indian
Head Nickel*

*2000 Sacagawea
Golden Dollar*

*2006 Buffalo
$50*

Pratt's 1908 Indian Head Quarter and Half Eagles marked a dramatic change in the way the Indian was depicted on American coins, from stylized symbolism to photorealism. The change was revolutionary, not evolutionary. The model for the face and his tribe is not known, but that he was a real person was made clear in Dr. Bigelow's comment that "the head was taken from a recent photograph of an Indian whose health was excellent" (Bigelow and Pratt furnished the photograph as proof).

James Earle Fraser followed Pratt's lead to create the powerful image of a realistic Indian chief (actually a composite of three to four different real Indians) on the 1913 Buffalo/Indian Head nickel.

Nearly 70 years passed before an Indian image again appeared on a U.S. coin made for circulation with the issue in 2000 of the Sacagawea "golden" dollar. The depiction by designer Glenna Goodacre of the young Indian guide for Lewis and Clark, though not actually photorealistic, is at least photorepresentative.

Ironically, Indians had been depicted realistically on American paper money many times on private bank notes prior to the establishment of a federal paper currency during the Civil War.

On regular issue U.S. currency, only one bill has borne an Indian image, the powerful and strikingly realistic portrayal by of Chief Ta-to-ka-inyanka (Running Antelope) on the 1899 "Indian Chief" $5 silver certificate. Even the dramatically naturalistic portrait by G.F.C. Smillie of the proud Indian chief

1899 $5 Silver Certificate designed by G.F.C. Smillie

took liberties with reality. The portrayal caused ill will among Indians because it depicted Chief Running Antelope, head of the Hunkpapa Sioux, wearing a Pawnee headdress. Not understanding the cultural implications, Smillie took artistic license because the original Sioux headdress with a single feather was not considered imposing enough or dramatic enough for the engraving.

It is said that Bela Lyon Pratt may have drawn inspiration for his design from the visual impact of Smillie's commanding image of a true Indian. For the first time on American coins, he got it right.

AMERICAN OR EUROPEAN EAGLE?

Quibbles by S. H. Chapman about the authenticity of the eagle shown on the reverse of the Pratt's design weren't Pratt's fault, according to Walter Breen. Chapman claimed the image looked more like a European golden eagle than an American bald or white-headed eagle (what qualified him as an expert on birds is not clear). Says Breen:

> "Chapman's major objection to the eagle was well-founded, but the blame is on [Charles] Barber, not Pratt; Pratt knew what a bald eagle looked like from working with models and photographs – otherwise Roosevelt would not have approved his design! – whereas Barber evidently did not."

Roosevelt was an avid outdoorsman and naturalist, having spent a number of years ranching in the North Dakota Badlands. He would certainly have spotted any major inaccuracies in Pratt's eagle depiction.

Besides, Pratt's eagle was a faithful derivative of the eagle on the reverse of Saint-Gaudens' $10 Eagle coin, which had been introduced a year earlier without controversy about the naturalistic accuracy of the bird's image.

If there was fault in the final product, it was apparently more evidence of mint engraver Charles Barber's incompetent tinkering with the design than of any deficiency in Pratt's eye for nature.

AMERCIAN EAGLE

EUROPEAN EAGLE

MATTE PROOF

The design wasn't the only controversial feature of the Indian Head Quarter and Half Eagle. A limited number of proof coins were struck for collectors using a new innovation not previously seen in U.S. coins until around 1908.

Instead of the bright, shiny mirror-like surface most collectors expected, the Mint used the matte proof technique popularized by the Paris Mint. The finish gave the surface a softer diffused finish (sandblast) with a uniform granular sheen meant to make the bright devices stand out stronger.

The actual method of producing the effect was a closely guarded secret, but experts believe the coins took several strikes from the press and then were "pickled" or etched in diluted acid.

While the innovative technique may have tickled the fancy of Charles Barber and his minions at the mint, the public turned up its nose. The matte proofs were unpopular because people didn't like the dull, flat finish and often couldn't distinguish them from common business strikes. Many were spent, either on purpose (during the Depression, for example) or by accident, and many more sat unwanted in government vaults until they were melted down.

ROMAN PROOF

In 1909 and 1910 the Mint produced a different finish proof referred to as Roman or Satin finish. The coins' look are often compared to a well stuck uncirculated specimen. The $2 1/2, $5, $10 and $20 gold pieces in those two years are typically seen with this finish.

THE PRATT-BIGELOW LEGACY

Pratt unequivocally broke new ground in American coin design. Yet his accomplishment was always overshadowed by the masterful work of his mentor Saint-Gaudens. Perhaps if his innovations had come before or well after Saint-Gaudens' beloved Eagle and Double Eagle classics, his work might have been treated differently. Saint-Gaudens was simply a tough act for anyone, no matter how talented, to follow.

The groundbreaking features that distinguished the Indian Head Quarter Eagle and Half Eagle never really captured the public imagination and thus had only limited impact on the course of American coin design. The incused relief concept has never been used again in

U.S. coinage. Photorealistic faces became the norm but, except for Fraser's Indian Head nickel, seldom with as much force and authority as Pratt's Indian chief. The matte proof finish and satin proof finish have appeared occasionally on other coins but with mixed reaction from collectors.

Nonetheless, history has been kinder to Pratt and his collaborator, Dr. Bigelow, than their contemporaries were. The Pratt-Bigelow legacy has been exonerated by time. Despite its less than auspicious beginnings, the Indian Head Quarter Eagle has earned its place as one of the most popular and sought-after of all American coins.

SIGNIFICANT PLAYERS OF THE
INDIAN HEAD QUARTER & HALF EAGLES

Knowing the plot only tells us part of the Indian Head Quarter and Half Eagle story. Knowing the characters fleshes out the story's dimensions, offering hints from their life experiences that may help explain why they did what they did and how they came to be involved in this story.

The cast of the Indian Head Quarter & Half Eagle drama includes some of the most interesting players in American numismatic history.

Theodore Roosevelt

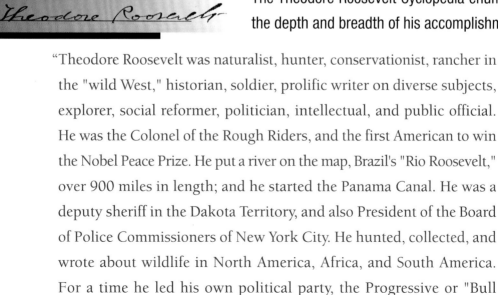

Easily one of the most colorful of all American presidents, Theodore Roosevelt has been called the Universal Man and the American Renaissance Man. Some historians hold up Benjamin Franklin and Thomas Jefferson as the only Americans in history to rival Roosevelt's multi-faceted character.

"Roosevelt was a many-sided man and every side was like an electric battery," said his friend and nature-writer John Burroughs. "Such versatility, such vitality, such thoroughness, such copiousness, have rarely been united in one man."

The Theodore Roosevelt Cyclopedia enumerated the depth and breadth of his accomplishments:

"Theodore Roosevelt was naturalist, hunter, conservationist, rancher in the "wild West," historian, soldier, prolific writer on diverse subjects, explorer, social reformer, politician, intellectual, and public official. He was the Colonel of the Rough Riders, and the first American to win the Nobel Peace Prize. He put a river on the map, Brazil's "Rio Roosevelt," over 900 miles in length; and he started the Panama Canal. He was a deputy sheriff in the Dakota Territory, and also President of the Board of Police Commissioners of New York City. He hunted, collected, and wrote about wildlife in North America, Africa, and South America. For a time he led his own political party, the Progressive or "Bull

Moose" Party. He was President of the American Historical Association. He was a major figure in American politics and government for nearly forty years. TR was elected to the New York State Assembly in 1881 at the age of twenty-three, and became President of the United States in 1901, at forty-two the youngest President before or since."

Roosevelt was born to a wealthy family in New York City on Oct. 27, 1858. He was sickly and asthmatic as a child, yet in spite of his poor health he was hyperactive and mischievous. His father made him exercise to help strengthen him and boxing lessons to deal with bullies.

He graduated from Harvard in 1876 and entered public life as a Republican activist, serving as a New York assemblyman.

Roosevelt's first wife and his mother both died on Valentine's Day 1884 in the same house, just two days after the birth of their only daughter, Alice. Roosevelt was devastated. He quit the General Assembly, gathered up his daughter and headed west to his ranch in the North Dakota badlands. He found the rugged life there as a rancher and lawman invigorating and healthful, convincing him of the value of the "strenuous life."

After the winter of 1886-87 wiped out his cattle and investment, he returned East to run for mayor of New York. Coming in a distant third, he traveled to London, where he married his childhood sweetheart Edith Kermit Carow. He was the only American chief executive to become a widower and remarry before becoming president.

Returning to Washington, the highly charismatic and larger than life Roosevelt began to make his mark in national politics, becoming Assistant Secretary of the Navy in 1887. At the outbreak of the Spanish-American War in Cuba in 1898, Roosevelt resigned from the Navy Department and formed the First U.S. Volunteer Cavalry Regiment, which the newspapers dubbed the "Rough Riders."

William McKinley won the election of 1900 with Roosevelt as his vice president. McKinley was shot by anarchist Leon Czolgosz on September 6, 1901. He died on September 14, making Roosevelt the nation's 26th and youngest president.

Nicknamed "Teddy" as a child, a name he detested, Roosevelt's informal moniker became attached to the popular children's stuffed bear toy after a hunting incident in 1902 when Roosevelt refused to shoot a black bear simply for the sake of making a kill. Whether he liked the name or not, the stuffed toy would be known from that point forward as the "teddy bear."

Roosevelt won the presidency in his own right in 1904. Roosevelt recognized, probably the first American president to do so, that the United States was destined to become a major world power. He saw it as America's duty to participate actively on the world stage and was the first to project American power abroad through the display of military might.

It was in this context of manifest destiny and Roosevelt's grand vision of America's emerging role of strength in the world that he sought to refine and elevate the nation's coinage to a stature worthy of a world power.

Dr. William Bigelow

Dr. William Sturgis Bigelow, one of the "Boston Brahmins"

Son of prominent Boston surgeon Dr. Henry Jacob Bigelow, William Sturgis Bigelow seemed ordained to follow in his famous father's footsteps. But he was to imprint his own deeply spiritual side on his career that would lead to his living in two distinct worlds.

Bigelow was born in 1850 to great privilege as one of the Boston Brahmins. The term Brahmin comes from the Indian caste system. The Brahmins are the highest caste in that social structure. Also called the First Families of Boston, the Brahmins are a blue-blooded class of New Englanders who claim hereditary or cultural lineage from the original Anglo-Saxon Protestants who founded the city of Boston and settled New England. They form the historic core of the so-called East Coast establishment, along with wealthy families of New York and Philadelphia. Among the Boston Brahmins were Samuel Adams, John Adams, John Quincy Adams, Henry Cabot Lodge, Percival Lowell and many other well-known lights of American culture (the Kennedys are not among the Brahmins).

William S. Bigelow graduated from Harvard Medical School in 1874 and continued his medical education in Europe, studying under Louis Pasteur. He returned to Boston to practice surgery at Massachusetts General Hospital.

But Bigelow wearied of his job and life in Boston and grew restless. He traveled to Japan with a friend and was immediately taken with the Japanese culture. He stayed for seven years, studying Japanese art and Buddhism, which became a lifelong study. His interest in Japanese art had grown even before he visited the country as he amassed a formidable collection. He donated more than 15,000 pieces and 40,000 prints to the Museum of Fine Arts in Boston in 1911.

It was through his involvement with the museum that he came to know Bela Lyon Pratt. It was also there that he saw and became enamored with the Egyptian art style of incuse sculpture, which later gave him the idea for the radical coin design that he suggested to his good friend Teddy Roosevelt.

When Dr. Bigelow died in 1926, he was split between two worlds, as he had been in life. Half his ashes were interred at the Mt. Auburn Cemetery in Cambridge, Massachusetts. The other half were buried in Japan near a Buddhist temple overlooking a lake he loved.

Bela Lyon Pratt

Bela Lyon Pratt was born on December 11, 1867 in Norwich, Connecticut to a family that prized education. His father was educated at Yale. His maternal grandfather founded a music conservatory in Connecticut.

Pratt entered Yale University's School of Fine Arts at age sixteen. His professors included celebrated artists John Henry Niemeyer and John Ferguson Weir. Three years later, Pratt was enrolled in the Art Students' League of New York, where his tutors included the likes of noted artists William Merritt Chase, Kenyon Cox, Francis Edwin Elwell, and Augustus Saint-Gaudens. Saint-Gaudens saw great promise in Pratt and became his mentor.

While working as Saint-Gaudens' assistant, Pratt gained admission to the prestigious Ecole des Beaux Arts in Paris, where he absorbed knowledge from renowned sculptors Henri-Michel-Antoine Chapu and Alexandre Falguière. Pratt won several medals and prizes while studying in Paris under the masters.

At Saint-Gaudens' invitation, he returned to Boston in 1892 to create two massive sculptural sets representing The Genius of Navigation for the 1893 World's Columbian Exposition in Chicago, thus launching his professional career.

He soon was offered the position as instructor of sculpture at the Boston Museum of Fine Arts (where he became acquainted with Dr. William Bigelow). He remained with the museum for 25 years.

In addition to his duties at the museum, Pratt maintained a private study to pursue his own works. There he produced numerous noteworthy sculptures which can now be found at the Library of Congress. He was awarded a silver medal at the 1901 Pan-American Exposition in Buffalo, New York.

Pratt is described as "a mild-mannered, modest, and congenial man who loved music and the outdoors." He married a sculpture student, Helen Pray. The couple had four children, and Pratt lived contentedly in a comfortable family setting.

Over the decades, he produced a wide-ranging array of work, including small portrait busts, reliefs, and memorial tablets to ideal nudes, fountain figures, and public monuments of "heroic size." He developed a technically skilled restrained naturalism in his work that some of his associates and contemporaries called "quintessentially American." No doubt it was this reputation that prompted Dr. Bigelow to seek out Pratt for the coin design project entrusted to him by President Roosevelt. The Indian Head Quarter and Half Eagles were the only coins Pratt designed. Undoubtedly he had had enough of the Mint bureaucracy and Charles Barber's meddling.

Charles Barber

Engraving ran in Charles Barber's family, though talent apparently did not. Barber's father William and grandfather John were engravers.Charles Edward Barber was born November 16, 1840 in London. William Barber emigrated with his family to the United States when Charles was 12. The elder Barber was appointed chief engraver of the U.S. Mint in 1869. Young Charles, by then 29, was apprenticed to his father at the Mint.

William Barber's dubious claim to fame is that during his tenure he was one of only two U.S. chief engravers of the 19th century who did not design a single major circulating coin. He died suddenly in 1879. President Rutherford B. Hayes appointed Charles Barber to fill his father's post as chief engraver of the Mint.

In contrast to his father, Charles Barber churned out a prodigious list of coins and medals, including the Barber dimes, quarters, and half dollars, and the Liberty Head "V" Nickel.

The latter was notable for the fact that Barber's first design, released into circulation in January 1883, did not carry the word CENTS anywhere on it. The Liberty design closely resembled the $5 gold piece then in circulation and was of similar size. Enterprising scoundrels plated the Liberty Head nickels with a thin layer of gold and passed them off as $5 coins. These became known as "racketeer nickels." Production had to be halted while Barber retooled the design to include the requisite word CENTS.

Numismatic historians differ in opinions about Barber's artistic merit. Though he has some defenders, they are in the minority. The predominant view generally holds that creatively he was colorless and unimaginative. His boring and predictable designs tended to regurgitate the tired conventions of antiquity and stuffiness of his native England. He was a man stuck in time, his visions gone out of fashion.

Underscoring the point, it was Barber who vigorously resisted the adoption of some of the most brilliantly creative coin designs in American history – those by Augustus Saint-Gaudens and Bela Lyon Pratt. His resistance can be laid in part to protecting his turf from outside intrusion. But it seems equally of import that Charles Barber very likely couldn't recognize a creative design if it was pasted to his nose.

It was precisely his lack of imagination and creativity that forced President Theodore Roosevelt to look outside the Mint for fresh ideas to begin with. Even upon direct orders from the president of the United States to make it happen, Barber did everything he possibly could to sabotage, deface, and demean three of the most beloved coin designs in U.S. coinage history. Despite his meddling and interference, the Saint-Gaudens' Eagle and Double Eagles, and Pratt's Quarter and Half Eagle masterpieces survived and endured. Charles Barber died February 18, 1917, in Philadelphia.

Frank Leach

Frank Aleomon Leach served as Director of the U.S. Mint from September 1907 to November 1909, filling the vacancy left by the departure of George E. Roberts. He had been at the time superintendent of the San Francisco Mint.

In that time frame, he had the difficult task of presiding over the contentious development of new coinage mandated by President Teddy Roosevelt using designers outside the jurisdiction of the Mint. Judging from his own writings, he was a reluctant buffer between the strong-willed, forceful Roosevelt and the stubborn, sulking Charles Barber. Leach's sympathies were clearly with his staff rather than with his boss.

Leach, a former newspaperman from California, detailed his view of the experience in a 1917 book, "Reflections of a Newspaper Man":

"Another very important matter was in hand in the bureau when I arrived at Washington, which was soon to cause me some anxiety, and that was the perfection of President Roosevelt's scheme for new designs for all the gold coins of our country. There were a number of prominent people in the East, especially in New York and Boston, who some time before began an agitation for an improvement in appearance of all our coinage. The President quickly became the leading spirit of the movement. The prevalent idea in this undertaking was that the design and execution of our coinage were inferior and inartistic when compared with those of ancient Greece; and as the coins used by a nation are one of the most enduring records of the art and mechanical skills of its age, our government should make an issue of coinage that would leave to future generations and ages something that would more truthfully and correctly reflect the artistic taste and mechanical ability of our day than the coinage then in use, unchanged for so many years. The admiration for the ancient Greek coins unwittingly influenced those gentlemen to suggestions that were imitative rather than original. They wanted the designs for the proposed coinage to be brought out in high relief, or with medallic effect, like the designs on the ancient coins. The commercial use and requirements seemed to have been lost sight of in the enthusiasm of producing a highly artistic coin; but in all probability none of the leading spirits in the movement was familiar with the use of metallic money, and did not understand that the proposed high relief would make the face of the coins so uneven that the pieces would not "stack," which was a condition fatal to the practicability of the idea."

As superintendent of the San Francisco Mint, Leach, a political appointee with no crisis management experience, along with 50 dedicated employees was instrumental in saving the Mint building from the devastating 1906 earthquake and fire that destroyed most of San Francisco. The small band of men fought desperately to preserve the building even as the flames melted the windows and burned the clothes from their backs. Incredibly, the Mint building was one of the few buildings left standing and stood as a symbol of survival to San Francisco as they rebuilt their ravaged city.

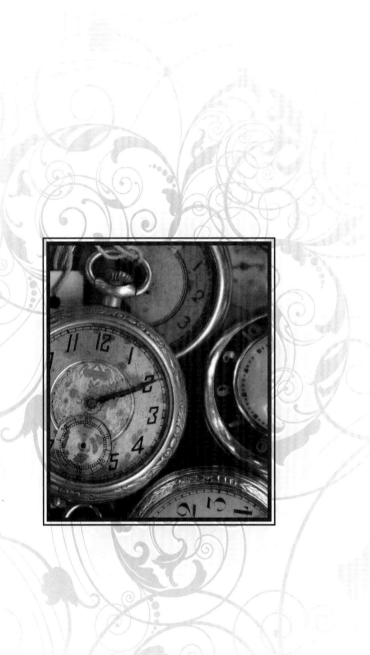

LIFE & TIMES OF THE INDIAN HEAD QUARTER & HALF EAGLES

When the Indian Head Quarter and Half Eagles began circulating in 1908, Oklahoma had just been admitted to the Union the previous year. Arizona and New Mexico would not become states for another four years.

At midnight on January 1, 1908, a ball dropped in New York's Times Square for the first time to signify the beginning of the new year. The famous Waldorf Thanksgiving dinner menu that year, according to the New York Evening Telegram Cook Book, offered "Cape Cod Oysters, Giblet Soup, Sheepshead with Hollandaise Sauce, Tomatoes Stuffed with Cucumbers, Saddle of New Jersey Mutton, Macedoine of Fresh Vegetables, Turkey Stuffed with Chestnuts, Cranberry Sauce, Brussels Sprouts, Potato Palestine, Lettuce and Grape Fruit Salad with Cracked Almonds, Plum Pudding with Rum Sauce, Mince and Pumpkin Pies, Glace Plombiere, Cafe."

Production of oil in the Middle East was just getting underway for the first time. In the U.S., Henry Ford produced the first Model T Ford. It sold for $850 (by 1925, the price had fallen to $290), putting the automobile in reach of the common man and ushering in the age of the automobile in America. By 1918, half the cars in the U.S. were Model T's.

The $2.50 Indian gold coin paid a day's wages for a worker in Ford's auto plant. Six years later, in 1914, Ford more than doubled wages, from $2.34 a day to $5, and reduced the workday to eight hours.

A postage stamp cost two cents in 1908. A Hershey Bar cost a nickel. Around that time a man's suit went for about $9, shirts for 30 to 70 cents, pants for $1.50 to $3 a pair, and socks three pairs for a quarter. Women's dress shoes ran about $4.25 a pair and a fur-lined coat could be had for $4.50.

Fancy creamery butter was about a 25 cents a pound, eggs 15 to 35 cents a dozen, sirloin beef steak three pounds for a quarter, ham 12 cents a pound. A dime would buy two jars of peanut butter or an 8 lb. bag of salt. Ketchup came dear at 75 cents a bottle. Farmers got 55 cents for a bushel of corn, 69 cents for barley, 47 cents for oats.

Cincinnati Mayor Mark Breith declared before the city council in 1908 that, "women are not physically fit to operate automobiles." A New York City ordinance made it illegal for a woman to smoke in public.

The year 1908 saw the first observance of Mother's Day, the first passenger flight in an airplane, the first horror movie (Dr. Jekyll and Mr. Hyde), the first U.S. postage stamps in rolls, the first federal workmen's compensation law, and the first U.S. credit union.

A race riot erupted in Springfield, Illinois. Bulgaria declared its independence from the Ottoman Empire. An earthquake near Messina, Italy, and the resulting tsunami killed 70,000 to 100,000 people in Italy and Sicily. A mysterious blast from a giant fireball, now believed to have been a piece of exploding comet, flattened more than a thousand square miles of forest at Tunguska, Siberia.

Tommy Burns knocked out Jem Roche in the fastest heavyweight title fight on record: 88 seconds. Nathan Stubblefield patented wireless radio broadcasting. Winston Churchill married Clementine Hozier. Robert Peary sailed from New York for his final assault on the North Pole. Serbia and Montenegro signed an anti-Austria-Hungarian pact, setting the stage for the First World War six years later. The passenger liner Lusitania, whose sinking in 1915 by a German U-boat's torpedo triggered America's entry into WWI, set an Atlantic crossing record of four days, 15 hours.

The year 1908 saw the birth of Edward Teller, father of the hydrogen bomb; economist John Kenneth Galbraith; Nazi hunter Simon Wiesenthal, American journalist Edward R. Murrow and English journalist Alistair Cooke; baseball announcer Red Barber; football coach Paul Brown, first coach of the Cleveland Browns named in his honor; cartoonist Tex Avery, creator of Bugs Bunny, Daffy Duck, and Droopy; Western novelist Louis L'Amour and James Bond creator Ian Fleming; comedians Milton Berle and Imogene Coca; composers Percy Faith and Leroy

Anderson; jazz great Lionel Hampton; and movie stars Jimmy Stewart, Rex Harrison, Bette Davis, Buddy Ebsen, Anna Magnani, Arthur O'Connell, and Carol Lombard.

By the time production of the $2½ and $5 Indian gold pieces ceased in 1929, Americans had survived the first global military conflict in history, the Roaring Twenties, Prohibition, Al Capone and the Mafia gang wars, and the opening days of what would become The Great Depression.

They were momentous times, and the Indian Head Quarter & Half Eagles were part of that historic panorama.

Holding an old gold coin in your hand is like holding a key that opens a door to the past. It's a physical connection to the life and times of the people who worked to earn the coin, carried it in their pockets or purses, and spent or saved it as they managed their money day to day. Learning about those times makes a coin come alive with the images and sounds of real people of another day.

The Indian Head Quarter and Half Eagles open a connection to the time of America growing up and coming of age.

A HISTORY OF THE $10 INDIAN HEAD EAGLES

A lunatic named Leon triggered (literally) the chain of events that produced one of the most cherished of all American gold coins – the Saint-Gaudens $10 Indian Head Eagle.

On September 6, 1901, at the Pan American Exposition in Buffalo, New York, crazed anarchist Leon Czolgosz sneaked in a .32 caliber revolver concealed in a handkerchief. At 4:07 p.m. when he reached the head of the receiving line to meet President William McKinley, Czolgosz fired two shots pointblank into the president. McKinley held onto life for more than a week, but died of his wounds on September 14.

The death of McKinley catapulted a feisty young Theodore Roosevelt into the presidency and the White House. That wasn't what the Republican Party had intended when they chose him to be McKinley's running mate in 1900.

Invigorated by "the strenuous life" of the North Dakota Badlands, the hard-charging young Teddy Roosevelt made the stuffy eastern Republicans uneasy. They were awed and somewhat intimidated by his raw, electrifying energy and bucking-bronc-loose-in-the-corral style of politics. They couldn't ignore the rampaging political aspirations of the commander

of the Rough Riders regiment in the Spanish-American War, the hero who led the charge up San Juan Hill in Cuba. So they chose the more sedate and malleable McKinley for their presidential candidate and stuck Roosevelt in the largely ceremonial role of vice president where they could hold him in check.

Czolgosz' two bullets changed everything, with far-reaching effects that included the complete overhaul of all American coinage design.

The Rough Rider Storms Washington

Teddy Roosevelt proved to be one of the most dynamic and effective presidents in American history, and he did it his way. The unstoppable Roosevelt built the Panama Canal, stamped out yellow fever in several countries, installed a new regime of public health, established the U.S. as a world naval power with the Great White Fleet, enforced a foreign policy of "Speak softly and carry a big stick," won the Nobel Peace prize…and totally reshaped the look of American coinage.

From the get-go, Teddy Roosevelt's forceful style challenged the entrenched conventions of hide-bound Washington. The strong-willed chief executive had his own way of doing things, and anyone who got in his way generally regretted the indiscretion.

Charles Barber, Chief Engraver at the U.S. Mint, would learn that lesson the hard way. Roosevelt was no fan of Barber and the other designers at the Mint. He considered them unimaginative hacks devoid of creative vision. When he won the presidency in his own right in 1904, Roosevelt rejected the trite design that Barber and George T. Morgan came up with for his inaugural medal.

Roosevelt discussed his displeasure over the lackluster medal design with an old friend, Frank Millet. Millet stated his opinion that the president would be better served not to rely on a commercial "journeyman" and instead summon the talents of a great artist worthy of the task. He recommended Boston sculptor Augustus Saint-Gaudens, sometimes called "The American Michelangelo" (Moran, 2003), to create a truly innovative medal design.

Roosevelt invited Saint-Gaudens to a luncheon attended by other lights of the time in arts and letters. During the luncheon, Saint-Gaudens was seated next to First Lady Edith Roosevelt, who admired his work greatly. No doubt she softened him up a bit for the president.

When Roosevelt brought up the medal proposition, Saint-Gaudens hesitated. The March deadline for the design was very tight, and he already had his plate full of work. Roosevelt might have dangled the prospect of getting the assignment to redesign United States coinage. So Saint-Gaudens suggested that he could oversee the medal design project even though he would not have time available to do the execution. He accepted the commission and sketched out a design on a paper napkin while on the train home from Washington. The famed sculptor turned over the task of modeling the actual design to his German-born associate, Adolph A. Weinman (The talented Weinman would later add to his renown by creating the superb Mercury dime and Walking Liberty half dollar).

The Saint-Gaudens/Weinman inaugural medal broke new ground in the aesthetics of presidential medals. "Saint-Gaudens' results shattered precedent," writes the Smithsonian Museum of American History. "The piece was modern in all senses of the word. There was no attempt to beautify or romanticize the President's head on the obverse, yet the image clearly conveyed vision and power. The reverse was, if anything, even more groundbreaking. The magnificent, left-facing eagle epitomized authority and presence, while displaying a classical ancient style…This bird unquestionably ruled all it surveyed."

Roosevelt was effusive in his praise for the result. He wrote to Saint-Gaudens:

Inaugural medal designed by Augustus Saint-Gaudens for President Theodore Roosevelt

> "My dear fellow, I am very grateful to you, and I am very proud to have been able to associate you in some way with my administration. I like the medals immensely; but that goes without saying; for the work is eminently characteristic of you."

Roosevelt added this handwritten personal note to the typed letter:

> Thank Heaven we have at last some artistic work of permanent worth done for the government. I don't want to slop over; but I feel just as if we had suddenly imported a little of Greece of the 5th or 4th centuries B.C. into America; and I am proud and grateful that I happen to be the beneficiary.

The medal met with such an enthusiastic reception that Roosevelt pressed on to enlist Saint-Gaudens as co-conspirator in what the president called his "pet crime" of revitalizing the artistic portfolio of American coin design. Saint-Gaudens was to create new designs for the cent, Eagle and Double Eagle coins.

Having bypassed the Mint staff for the medal design, Roosevelt further snubbed the bureaucrats by having the medal struck, not at the U.S. Mint in Philadelphia as usual, but at Tiffany & Co. in New York. The rebuff ruffled feathers in Philadelphia anew and added sinew to the campaign of resistance that was to bedevil Roosevelt and Saint-Gaudens later.

Birth of a Coin Design Renaissance

Roosevelt loathed the appearance of American coins. With the subject of going outside the usual channels for artistic talent for a medal design broached and deemed a viable option, Roosevelt started mulling the possibility of doing the same for coin designs. At the end of December 1904, he inquired of Secretary of the Treasury Leslie Shaw:

> "I think our coinage is artistically of atrocious hideousness. Would
> it be possible, without asking permission of Congress, to employ
> a man like Saint-Gaudens to give us a coinage of some beauty?"

Roosevelt and Saint-Gaudens shared the view that existing coin design in America was "timid, old-fashioned, and ugly." (Rose, 2004) American coin design was also stagnating. The look of the penny hadn't been changed in forty years, the Double Eagle had looked the same for sixty years, and the Eagle, Half-Eagle, and Quarter-Eagle had carried their same designs for nearly seventy years.

The president and the artist both greatly admired the high-relief coins of classic antiquity, especially the dramatic raised designs on coins of ancient Greece and the bold Renaissance medals of Pisanello and Sperandio. As the two friends huddled together one cold November night in 1905 at the White House sharing ideas, they grew more and more excited over their vision of coin designs of such aesthetic grandeur that they would be hailed with critical acclaim around the world. Their voices grew more animated as their enthusiasm swelled, caught up in the feverish creative energy of the moment.

The momentous climax of the evening came when President Roosevelt declared that, if Saint-Gaudens would create the designs, he would force the Mint to produce them whether they liked it or not. Saint-Gaudens accepted the challenge, even knowing he had little time left to live. Cancer was draining the life from him. He would have to hurry.

That night marked the birth of a coin design renaissance that ushered in the Golden Age of American coinage.

OVERCOMING THE BAD TASTE OF A MINT

Augustus Saint-Gaudens set to work with a will fired by his zeal for the president's vision and with an urgency driven by his failing health. He recognized that he was the chosen instrument of an historic epiphany for coin aesthetics in America.

At his studio in Cornish, New Hampshire, the ailing master sculptor feverishly sketched concepts for new designs. He corresponded frequently with President Roosevelt as the two friends exchanged ideas, defining, refining, and amplifying their original inspiration.

At one point in these exchanges, Saint-Gaudens couldn't resist a jibe at the Mint drones at whose hands he had previously suffered indignities. "Whatever I produce cannot be worse than the inanities now displayed on our coins," he wrote to Roosevelt.

Saint-Gaudens had good reason to disdain Charles Barber and the Mint Bureau. He had been subjected to their creative incompetence and bureaucratic obtuseness on two unhappy occasions before.

In 1891, Saint-Gaudens served on a judging committee to evaluate designs for new silver coins. None submitted were deemed acceptable because the best artists had boycotted the competition in protest over the meager prize offered for the winning design. Saint-Gaudens was appalled when Charles Barber regurgitated a near mirror-image copy of a George Morgan design and presented it as an "improvement" over the submitted designs.

Though soured by his disagreeable first encounter with government mediocrity, Saint-Gaudens nonetheless soon afterward accepted a commission to create the official medal for the 1892 World's Columbian Exposition. The design he submitted portrayed a naked Grecian youth holding a torch and victors' wreaths on the reverse.

A firebrand named Anthony Comstock, the hypocritical founder of the Society for the Suppression of Vice – and reputedly the owner of the second largest collection of pornography in the world, according to numismatic historian Walter Breen – raised such a stink about the nude figure on the medal that Saint-Gaudens withdrew the design for the reverse. Charles Barber was asked to come up with a replacement design, which turned out to be predictably banal.

Disgusted and infuriated by the revolting affair, Saint-Gaudens swore he would go to his grave before he would ever have any dealings with the Mint Bureau again. He held true to his vow for 14 years.

Only the compelling magnetism of Teddy Roosevelt and the artist's enthusiasm for his friend's grand purpose persuaded him to relent and try once more. He only did so with the expectation that Roosevelt would be his champion and protector in his dealings with the Mint. "If you succeed in getting the best of the polite Mr. Barber...or others in charge," Saint-Gaudens wrote to the president, "you will have done a greater work than putting through the Panama Canal. Nevertheless, I shall stick to it, even unto death."

His words proved prophetic. Saint-Gaudens died before seeing his visionary new coin designs in circulation.

For their part, Charles Barber and the Mint made this experience almost as disagreeable for Saint-Gaudens as the ones preceding it.

A TRIUMPH OF SPIRIT

At every opportunity, Charles Barber threw roadblocks and speed bumps in front of the project, procrastinating and fussing about design details and generally being obstructive. He was a third-generation bureaucrat well-schooled in the art of mucking up the government works for his own ends.

Yet despite the Mint's intransigent pigheadedness, relentless meddling, and determined efforts to sabotage the project, Saint-Gaudens persevered to emerge the spiritual victor with two of the most revered coin designs in United States history (and, some say, in the history of world coinage) – the transcendent Double Eagle and exquisite Indian Head Eagle that bear his name to this day. (Saint-Gaudens also produced preliminary models for a new cent design, but the work was set aside as his health ebbed. The design was never completed.)

The $10 Indian Head Eagle portrayed a classic profile of Lady Liberty wearing an Indian headdress – added at the insistence of President Roosevelt – on the obverse and a magnificent standing eagle on the reverse.

The first Indian Head Eagles were produced in 1907, and the coin continued to circulate with various modifications minted in Philadelphia, Lower relief Indian Head Eagle coins were produced by the mints at Philadelphia, Denver, and San Francisco until the denomination ceased production by presidential executive order by Teddy Roosevelt's cousin Franklin D. Roosevelt in 1933.

Today the $10 Indian Head eagle reigns as one of the most desirable masterworks from the Golden Age of U.S. coin design, coveted by collectors for its extraordinary beauty and elusive rarity.

DESIGN DETAILS OF THE $10 INDIAN HEAD EAGLES

The Indian Head Eagle is misnamed. The principal feature that gives the coin its name is not the face of an Indian, nor is the feathered headdress an accurate portrayal of any tribal trappings of American Indians.

WHEN IS AN INDIAN NOT AN INDIAN?

For the obverse, Saint-Gaudens used for the face of Lady Liberty an adaptation almost identical to the Nike (Victory) head he had sculpted for the Sherman Monument in New York's Central Park (which just happened to be First Lady Edith Roosevelt's favorite work of his). That figure was in turn inspired by the image of a Hellenist Wingless Victory in the temple of Zeus among the ruins of the ancient Greek city-state of Pergamon.

However, the original laurel crown was replaced with a handsome but entirely fictitious Indian war bonnet. That was the president's idea, as described by numismatic historian Walter Breen:

> "At Pres. Roosevelt's insistence, and for no other reason, St. Gaudens gave this head a nationalistic character by the absurd addition of a feathered warbonnet, such as neither Ms. Liberty nor any Native American woman would ever have worn. And so this new design acquired the misleading sobriquet of 'Indian Head,' properly applicable only to Pratt's 1908-29 Half Eagles and Quarter Eagles. Possibly the warbonnet also served to conceal any connection with the Sherman monument, to minimize protests in the South."

Though it was overtly an affectation, Saint-Gaudens offered no objections and even applauded the idea. On March 12, 1907, he wrote to Roosevelt:

> "I like so much the head with a headdress (and by the way, I am very glad you suggested doing the head in that manner) that I should like to see it tried not only on the cent piece but also on the twenty-dollar gold piece, instead of the figure of Liberty."

The word LIBERTY is inscribed on the headband of the war bonnet, with an arch of thirteen stars above and the date below the head. The model for the profile was Alice Butler, who posed for other works by Saint-Gaudens.

THE MARY CUNNINGHAM FLAP

A brief but interesting flap erupted when rumors circulated that the model for the decidedly American coin was in fact a foreigner!   In a time when image of "The American Girl," the ideal American lass, was all the rage, using a foreign face on a U.S. coin would have been considered political and social heresy. (Bowers, 2001)

Word spread that the model for the face on the $10 Eagle was that of one Mary Cunningham, an Irish immigrant waitress at an "eating house" in the town of Cornish, Vermont, across the river from Saint-Gaudens' studio in Cornish, New Hampshire.

Since Saint-Gaudens was no longer around to clarify the identity of the model, the controversy escalated to the point of protests reportedly being lodged with the Secretary of Treasury. According to historian Q. David Bowers, numismatist Edgar H Adams posted an item in the New York Sun with this comment:

> "A Pennsylvania Society has protested against the act of the late Augustus Saint-Gaudens in using as the design for the new coin the profile of a young woman born out of the United States. It is interesting to reflect that the model used for long by another artist for his typical 'American girl' was also an alien."

Mary Cunningham was pure fiction. No such person was ever involved in the development of the $10 Indian Head Eagle design.

IMPERIAL EAGLE

For the reverse, Saint-Gaudens reprised the powerful standing eagle he had created for Roosevelt's inaugural medal. It is almost identical.

Presumably the thought might have been that only a relative handful of people could enjoy the image on the inaugural medals, but emblazoning it on a coin would make it accessible to the masses (of course, most of the masses of the day seldom saw anything as rich as a $10 coin).

The left-facing eagle echoes the style of the imperial eagle that was a common theme on Ptolemaic Egyptian and imperial Roman coin. The eagle is perched on a bundle of arrows with an olive branch (peace and preparedness for war). The motto E PLURIBUS UNUM is tucked in to the right by the bird's neck, with UNITED STATES OF AMERICA arching overhead and the denomination TEN DOLLARS below.

"IN GOD WE TRUST" CONTROVERSY

The most controversial aspect of the original Indian Head Eagle design was what it did not include. The motto IN GOD WE TRUST was missing.

As the result of a surge in religious sentiment growing out of a brutal Civil War, the motto had been inscribed on U.S. coinage beginning with the two-cent coin in 1864. The motto was not included on all coins and not continuously used on some that once had it. There was no law preventing its omission.

The Eagle was one of the coins which had borne the motto since being authorized by the Congressional Act of March 3, 1865. Its absence from the new Indian Head Eagle stirred an uproar from the religious community.

It's ironic that it was for reasons of piety that the motto had been omitted. Roosevelt and Saint-Gaudens, both devout men, believed it an act of blasphemy to imprint the hallowed phrase on money that may be used for sinful purposes, such as gambling or prostitution. Roosevelt explained his view in a November 11, 1907, letter to William Boldly:

> "My own feeling in the matter is due to my very firm conviction that to put such a motto on coins, or to use it in any kindred manner, not only does no good but does positive harm, and is in effect irreverence, which comes dangerously close to sacrilege…It is a motto which it is indeed well to have inscribed on our great national monuments, in our temples of justice, in our legislative halls, and in building such as those at West Point and Annapolis — in short, wherever it will tend to arouse and inspire a lofty emotion in those who look thereon. But it seems to me eminently unwise to cheapen such a motto by use on coins, just as it would be to cheapen it by use on postage stamps, or in advertisements."

reverse

| 1908-D | 1908-D |
| WITH MOTTO | NO MOTTO |

The public wasn't buying Roosevelt's rationale and besieged the White House and Congress with protests about "TR's godless coins." When it became clear that Congress was going to move on reinstating the motto, Roosevelt replied to Montana Senator Thomas Carter regarding a statement about the matter in a House committee:

> "The Congressman says the House Committee wants to pass a bill restoring the motto to the coin. I tell him it is not necessary; it is rot; but the Congressman says there is a misapprehension as to the religious purport of it — it is so easy to stir up a sensation and misconstrue the President's motive — and that the Committee is agitated as to the effect of a veto. I repeat, it is rot, pure rot; but I am telling the Congressman if Congress wants to pass a bill reestablishing the motto, I shall not veto it. You may as well know it in the Senate also."

Congress passed a bill in May 1908 prescribing as follows:

> "Be it enacted by the Senate and House of Representatives of the United States of America in Congress assembled, That the motto "In God We Trust," heretofore inscribed on certain denominations of the gold and silver coins of the United States of America, shall hereafter be inscribed upon all such gold and silver coins of said denominations as heretofore."

As he had promised, Roosevelt signed the act on May 18, 1908.

MIXED PUBLIC REACTION

Apart from the religious controversy, public reaction to the new design was lukewarm at first, but people warmed to the coin after they got over the dramatic change from the ordinary coinage most had known all their lives.

The Indian Head Eagle generally was applauded by the numismatic community on its aesthetic merits.

Howland Wood. secretary of the American Numismatic Association, wrote in The Numismatist (December 1907):

> "The coin is a magnificent conception throughout, of a refined Greek character, simple in its aspect, but grand in its dignity, and will surely find a place in the front rank with the best coins of the age."

Charles Connick of Boston wrote in November 1907 to The Elder Monthly:

> "It is not strange that a feeling of exultation results from one's first glimpse of the new $10 gold coin. Chagrin and dismay have long stirred within us at sight of our coins in contrast with these of other nations, and to have one now that need not be defended save from attacks of patriotic committees from Harrisburg [from whence the Mary Cunningham protest emanated] and from over-zealous religious enthusiasts, is indeed gratifying."

The acclaim was not, however, unanimous. New York numismatist Ebenezer Gilbert fumed, "The coin, both obverse and reverse, is a humiliating disappointment, without one redeeming feature, and is a 'foozle [a stupid, clumsy mistake]." Gilbert fussed about proportions and placement of elements. He referred to the eagle on the reverse as "a turkey buzzard in pantalets."

Gilbert's was a minority opinion, however, and the $10 Indian Head eagle soon swelled in popularity.

1933 Issue Confusion

Numismatic researcher and writer Richard Giedroyc noted in "The History Of The United States $10 Gold Piece" that collectors sometimes get mixed up regarding the 1933 issue of the Indian Head eagle. Said Giedroyc:

> "There is considerable confusion regarding the 1933 Indian Head Eagle. Some of the coins were legally released prior to the executive order stopping the release of all U.S. gold coins. Some collectors confuse these difficult to find coins with the 1933 Saint-Gaudens $20 double eagle coin which is illegal to own since none of them were legally released prior to the same executive order."

Today, one 1933 $20 is legal to own and sold auction for an all time record of $7,590,020. Other 1933 $20's are the subject of a legal challenge.

Beauty Dimmed But Not Damned by Bureaucrat's Butchery

Even President Roosevelt's strong arm could not completely protect the beauty of Saint-Gaudens' Indian Head eagle design from Charles Barber's ham-fisted butchery.

Through a series of experimental strikes, Barber found various excuses to tinker with this and that detail of the design and muddle it with his singularly dense incompetence (the one thing Barber was really good at is mediocrity).

Walter Breen charged that "the design finally put into circulation is not by St. Gaudens at all, but is instead Barber's inferior copy of the St. Gaudens models." The relief was less bold. Triangular dots bracketing UNITED STATES OF AMERICA were eliminated. The eagle's olive branch got a different shape. Other details were altered.

In the end, though, even Barber's bumbling buffoonery could not extinguish the creative brilliance displayed in Saint-Gaudens' work. The drama and grace at the core of the inspired design defied all efforts to deface it as the true artistic spirit shone through.

SIGNIFICANT PLAYERS OF THE $10 INDIAN HEAD EAGLES

Knowing the names of the characters in this story tells us the who but not the why of the people involved with events that produced the Indian Head Eagle. As we learn more about them as individuals, we gain deeper understanding of the motivations that make sense of their words and deeds.

The tale of the Indian Head Eagle is populated with colorful characters of such divergent nature it would seem improbable that they would find any commonality. Yet here they are, all part of the same story and forever inseparable in history's chronicles.

THEODORE ROOSEVELT

Theodore Roosevelt, Jr., 25th vice president and 26th president of the United States, came to the White House as the youngest president in American history.

Surveys of scholars over the years consistently rank "T.R." from third to seventh on the list of America's greatest presidents. He has been called "the most interesting American." He brought a can-do dynamism to the chief executive office at precisely the time in history when the United States was poised to take its place as a leading player on the world stage.

Historian Thomas Bailey said of him, "Roosevelt was a great personality, a great activist, a great preacher of the moralities, a great controversialist, a great showman. He dominated his era as he dominated conversations....the masses loved him; he proved to be a great popular idol and a great vote getter."

Roosevelt the man was a contrast to Roosevelt the boy. Born of wealthy parents in New York on October 27, 1858 – he was three years old when the Civil War broke out – young Roosevelt was a sickly child, plagued by asthma and poor health. Yet despite his fragility, the rambunctious spirit that would characterize his later life showed through. He was hyperactive and mischievous.

Roosevelt the Senior urged his frail son into activities that would strengthen him, enrolling him for boxing lessons and building a home gym for his workouts. By the time young Roosevelt entered Harvard in 1876, he was quite athletic and participated actively in varsity sports. He was runner-up in the Harvard boxing championship. He would be a lifelong advocate of "the strenuous life" as a means to vigorous health.

His early struggles as a child imbued Roosevelt with a drive to overcome obstacles, an indomitable will to win that set the course for the rest of his life. He believed he could accomplish whatever he set his mind to…and did.

"Roosevelt was a many-sided man and every side was like an electric battery," said his friend and nature-writer John Burroughs. "Such versatility, such vitality, such thoroughness, such copiousness, have rarely been united in one man."

Roosevelt historian John Allen Gable, who described Roosevelt as the "universal man," summarized highlights of Roosevelt's accomplishments thus:

Theodore Roosevelt was a naturalist, hunter, conservationist, rancher in the "wild West," historian, soldier, prolific writer on diverse subjects, explorer, social reformer, politician, intellectual, and public official. He was the Colonel of the Rough Riders, and the first American to win the Nobel Peace Prize. He put a river on the map, Brazil's "Rio Roosevelt," over 900 miles in length; and he started the Panama Canal. He was a deputy sheriff in the Dakota Territory, and also President of the Board of Police Commissioners of New York City. NRA Life member, Roosevelt hunted, collected, and wrote about wildlife in North America, Africa, and South America. For a time he led his own political party, the Progressive or "Bull Moose" Party. He was President of the American Historical Association. He was a major figure in American politics and government for nearly forty years. TR was elected to the New York State Assembly in 1881 at the age of twenty-three, and became President of the United States in 1901, at forty-two the youngest President before or since.

Graduating from Harvard in 1880 (magna cum laude and Phi Beta Kappa), Roosevelt pursued law studies at Columbia University. He found law boring, though, and in 1882 set about writing his first book, The Naval War of 1812, still considered the definitive work on the topic.

The energetic and charismatic Roosevelt seemed drawn to politics as a bear to honey. He quit school to run for New York Assemblyman, launching a long and stellar public career that led eventually to the White House. Were it not for his extraordinary will, Roosevelt might never have made a notable mark on history. He was devastated by the death of his father and subsequently of his mother and first wife (who both died on the same day – Valentine's Day 1884). The disconsolate Roosevelt drew a big "X" in his diary and wrote, "The light has gone out of my life."

He packed up his daughter Alice and moved west, to North Dakota, to flee the painful memories. There the rugged, robust life of a rancher and lawman revitalized his spirit, filling him with a renewed zest for tackling hard challenges.

After the severe winter of 1886-87 wiped out his cattle herd and his investment, Roosevelt returned to the East to resume what he loved most – politics. He ran for mayor of New York City, finishing a distant third.

After the unsuccessful campaign, he traveled to London, married his childhood friend Edith, and climbed Mont Blanc, the highest Alpine peak in Western Europe.

Feeling no mountain of adversity could stop him, Roosevelt returned to the States and applied himself with characteristic vigor to making waves in politics, getting him noticed by the kingmakers of the Republican party. His ambitions to be president got put on hold when the party chose to pair him with William McKinley for the 1900 election, not as candidate for president but as vice president. Roosevelt knew the largely ceremonial second banana job was a political graveyard and considered his career finished. He contemplated returning to law school.

Leon Czolgosz handed him another chance to fulfill his destiny by gunning down McKinley in 1901, thus handing Roosevelt the coveted office he thought had eluded him. Roosevelt seized the moment and never looked back. He knew instinctively that he was in the right place at the right time with the right talents to guide America's emergence as a world power to be reckoned with.

His vision of manifest destiny informed his every decision, including the total renovation of America's sovereign signature as projected in the imagery on the nation's coinage.

AUGUSTUS SAINT-GAUDENS

In many respects, Augustus Saint-Gaudens was Roosevelt's opposite number, the yin to Roosevelt's yang. Where Roosevelt was outgoing and forceful, Saint-Gaudens was more reserved and sensitive (though said to have a warm personality that attracted many friends). Roosevelt reveled in the public arena, while Saint-Gaudens shied from it, at least where the government was involved. Roosevelt was born to privilege and power; Saint-Gaudens was the son of an immigrant shoemaker.

Yet the two men found common ground on two significant points: 1) They both believed America's coinage needed a dramatic makeover, and 2) both were convinced the U.S. Mint was not up to the task.

The two intellectual giants held each other in high mutual respect. They quickly became loyal friends as they joined forces in their quest to place American coinage on a world pedestal. Saint-Gaudens was born in Dublin, Ireland, in1848, inauspiciously at the height of the Irish Potato Famine. His father, Bernard, was shoemaker from a small village in the French Pyrenees who moved first to London then to Dublin, where he married Mary McGuinness. Six months after Augustus was born, the family immigrated to New York City

At 13, Augustus was apprenticed to a French cameo-cutter in New York. He went to art school at night and later studied at the National Academy of Design near his home. At 19, his father offered him a chance to see the Exposition of 1867 in Paris. While in Paris, Saint-Gaudens got work assisting an Italian cameo-cutter while he waited to be accepted to the famous French art school Ecole des Beaux-Arts. In 1870, Saint-Gaudens left Paris for a five-year sojourn in Rome, where he honed his art skills while expanding his international circle of friends.

He returned to America at age 27 and straight away won a commission in 1876 to design a statue of Civil War admiral David G. Farragut. It was a crucial turning point in his life, earning him both national recognition and the financial security to marry Augusta Homer, whom he had met while in Rome. She was a cousin of famed American artist Winslow Homer.

His success with the Farragut commission secured Saint-Gaudens future, leading to a steady succession of important public works, each one adding measure to his renown. He earned acclaim as America's premier sculptor.

In gratitude to those who had instructed him in his craft, Saint-Gaudens in turn took great pains to encourage the artists who would follow him. He taught at the Art Students League and privately tutored promising artists. He became a leader among his artist peers and helped found the Society of American Artists.

The Farragut Memorial
in Madison Square Park

His popularity among his peers was such that many prominent creative cognoscenti followed him to Cornish, New Hampshire, where his studio was, thus forming what became known as the "Cornish Colony." Among them were painters Maxfield Parrish, Thomas Dewing, George Deforest Brush, and Kenyon Cox, dramatist Percy MacKaye, the American novelist Winston Churchill, architect Charles Platt, and sculptors Paul Manship and Louis Saint-Gaudens (Augustus' brother).

He was an accessible and willing supporter of artistic causes. It was his willingness to serve in such causes that he first suffered the bitter taste of dealing with nincompoops in public life. A sour experience while serving on a judging committee in 1891 to evaluate designs for new silver coins repelled him from being involved with government projects. It was the first time he encountered the dullard Charles Barber, but it would not be the last.

His conflicts with Charles Barber dogged Saint-Gaudens until he died of cancer in 1907.

CHARLES BARBER

It has been said that Charles E. Barber probably designed more medals and coins than any other person ever employed by the United States government. What he lacked in quality of talent he made up for in quantity of output. Barber was a third-generation engraver of the English old school, and it showed in his work. His designs looked dated and antique when they were brand new, basically frozen in time from an earlier age.

He did have one skill at which he excelled, however – working the system of bureaucracy. Like his father and his father's father, Charles Barber was a professional government minion.

His father, William, brought the family to the U.S. in 1852 when Charles was 12. The elder Barber was appointed Chief Engraver at the U.S. Mint in 1869. Young Charles, then 29, was apprenticed to his father at the Mint.

When William Barber died in 1879, President Rutherford B. Hayes nominated Charles Barber to succeed his father as chief engraver. The Senate confirmed his appointment on January 20, 1880. Since the Philadelphia Mint was the oldest in the country and had the only official United States government engraving department, the position commanded great prestige as a direct presidential appointment.

Barber was nothing if not prolific. During his career at the Mint, he produced, among others, these coin designs:

- 1892-1916 "Barber" series of dimes, quarters, and half dollars
- 1883-1912 Liberty Head Nickel
- 1892-93 Columbian Exposition half dollar (reverse)
- 1900 Lafayette dollar
- 1903 Louisiana Purchase gold dollar
- 1904 Lewis and Clark Exposition gold dollar
- 1915 Panama-Pacific Exposition Quarter Eagle and 50-cent piece
- 1916 McKinley Memorial gold dollar.

He also created coinage for Hawaii and Cuba. In addition, Barber designed some 29 different medals, including portrait medals, lifesaving medals, inauguration medals, and American Indian peace medals, and the U.S. Grant peace medal. He did presidential portrait designs for Garfield, Arthur, Cleveland, and Harrison.

Unfortunately, all that practice only perfected his banality and introduced no new inspiration of creative genius. Barber's total portfolio looks almost uniformly tired and lifeless.

Certainly there was nothing in his vast body of work that impressed President Teddy Roosevelt, least of all the prosaic inaugural medal design he and George Morgan proposed to the newly-elected president. Roosevelt was underwhelmed by their effort and sought better talent elsewhere.

Barber was humiliated and incensed by the rebuff. He was unaccustomed to being dismissed so cavalierly. He may have harbored illusions of standing up to the president, relying on his network of crony contacts to work the system to his own end. But he hadn't reckoned on running up against the iron will of Teddy Roosevelt.

Barber deeply resented the incursion on his turf of design talent from outside the Mint. He resented being dictated to by the president, even if the chief executive was his boss. When forced against his will to execute the designs of artists outside his control, Barber used every machination he could invent to impede, corrupt, and sabotage the interloper coin projects.

It would undoubtedly deepen his bitterness if he knew that today he is remembered as a hero by few and a villain by many. Barber is mostly remembered today not so much for the works he created himself but for his role in obstructing the Golden Age of U.S. coin design, for trying to quash or at least vandalize the works of others that became some of the most beautiful coin designs in American history.

FRANK LEACH

Frank A. Leach found himself thrust into a nasty bureaucratic tangle when he took up his new post as Director of the U.S. Mint in November 1909. He arrived not long after the beginning of President Theodore Roosevelt's foray into numismatic adventurism, a period perceived as a crisis of confidence within the mint system.

Leach had proved his mettle in crisis management only a few years earlier during the great 1906 earthquake in San Francisco.

Leach was editor and publisher of the evening Enquirer in Oakland, California, when he was selected in August 1897 to be superintendent of the San Francisco Mint. In just 10 years, he had built the newspaper from a semi-weekly advertising sheet to powerful daily with considerable political clout.

No doubt it was his political influence that landed Leach the job heading up the Mint. He had no prior experience running a mint operation.

Nine years later, at 5:13 on the morning of April 18, 1906, Leach was jolted awake by the noises of protest from his violently shaking home in Oakland, which was, in his words, "dancing a lively jig." When the shaking stopped, he hurriedly dressed and headed for the Mint in San Francisco, not yet aware of the devastation in the city. When he could see across the bay, he was stunned to see the pall of black smoke blanketing the city.

Struggling to overcome the crush of panic, debris, and chaos that impeded his path, he made his way to the Mint building. He was relieved to find the building intact and undamaged. However, the Mint was threatened by approaching fires that had already leveled several blocks around the building.

Leach quickly organized the 50 or so employees on duty along with 10 soldiers to mount a defense against the fire. They removed anything flammable they could find, then rigged boiler pumps to water hoses to wet the building down, assisted by manual bucket brigades. They battled the fire until the building was secured about 5:00 o'clock that afternoon. It was one of the few buildings left standing in San Francisco.

As difficult as it was, saving the San Francisco Mint from the earthquake fires may have seemed to Frank Leach an easy task when measured against taming the flames of conflict he inherited when he took charge of the national mint system.

Leach described in his *Recollections of a Newspaperman* the circumstances he encountered when he arrived in Washington to assume the post vacated by George E. Roberts:

> "Another very important matter was in hand in the bureau when I
> arrived at Washington, which was soon to cause me some anxiety, and
> that was the perfection of President Roosevelt's scheme for new
> designs for all the gold coins of our country. There were a number
> of prominent people in the East, especially in New York and Boston,
> who some time before began an agitation for an improvement in
> appearance of all our coinage. The President quickly became the
> leading spirit of the movement."

Leach found himself soon enough in the unenviable and thankless role of mediator between the strong-willed chief executive and the sullen, restive mint staff.

His sympathies were clearly and understandably with his own staff, yet he was astute enough in political practicalities to know he had to fulfill his boss' wishes or he would quickly be jobless. He negotiated and wheedled compromises on both sides of the conflict to get the contested coin designs moved to completion. By his own account, the president approved of his handling of the job:

> "I certainly believed him when he declared he was 'delighted.' He
> warmly congratulated me on my success, and was most complimentary
> in his comments."

Frank Leach held the post of Mint Director until November 1909.

LIFE & TIMES OF THE $10 INDIAN HEAD EAGLES

In 1907 when the $10 Indian first began circulating, bubonic plague broke out in San Francisco, while in Seattle the now-famed Pike Place Market opened and Jim Casey founded UPS (United Parcel Service). James Spangler invented the Hoover vacuum cleaner (Spangler's first customer was his cousin, who was married to William Hoover, who bought into Spangler's company, became president, and renamed the company). Oklahoma became the 46th state. Florenz Ziegfield staged the first of his legendary music extravaganzas in the "Ziegfield Follies." Charles Curtis of Kansas became the first Native American U.S. senator. J.P. Morgan and other Wall Street poobahs averted a major financial crisis by investing $25 million to prop up stocks on the panic-stricken New York Stock Exchange. A coal mine explosion in Pennsylvania killed 239.

Federal spending topped out at $0.58 billion (today it's more than 600 times that much). Unemployment was only 2.8%. A first-class stamp cost two cents. Elsewhere in the world, thieves made off with the Irish crown jewels and outlaws pulled off the one and only train robbery in Sweden's history. The first cabs with taxi meters appeared in London. Korea became a protectorate of Japan, and the U.S. claimed a protectorate over the Dominican Republic. An earthquake in Jamaica killed more than 1,000 people. Maria Montessori opened her first school and daycare center in Rome. The first commercial color photography process – Autochrome Lumiere – was marketed in France. The Second Hague Peace Conference adopted international rules of war. French bicycle dealer Paul Cornu flew the first helicopter that could carry a human (it crashed on landing after a 20-second flight).

The year 1907 gave the world Russian rocket scientist Sergei Korolev, Japanese Nobel laureate physicist Hideki Yukawa, and Scottish Nobel laureate chemist Baron Alexander Todd. The year also saw the births of English author Dame Daphne du Maurier and American science fiction writer Robert Heinlein and a banner crop of future entertainers: John Wayne and Katherine Hepburn (who teamed in the classic movie "Rooster Cogburn" nearly 70 years later in 1975); Robert Young ("Father Knows Best"); Buster Crabbe ("Tarzan"); Fay Wray ("King Kong"); Gene Autry, the singing cowboy and future owner of the Los Angeles Angels baseball franchise; actor, writer, director, and producer Sheldon Leonard; English actor and director Sir Laurence Olivier; along with Burgess Meredith, Barbara Stanwyck, Cesar Romero, and Pinky Lee.

Rudyard Kipling ("Gunga Din") won the Nobel prize in literature. Norwegian composer Edvard Greig ("In the Hall of the Mountain King") died.

According to prices listed in the Morris County, New Jersey, Daily Record in December 1911, a $10 Indian would buy 10 men's dress shirts or more than a dozen silk neckties. Two of the coins would buy a man's suit or three women's dresses. You could rent a six-room house with a modern bath and steam heat for $25, but if you were willing to live near a train station, you could get a place for $16. You could furnish your home for $8 with an enameled bed ($21 if you wanted a brass bed), $5 apiece for Morris-style golden oak chairs with tufted cushions, $10 for a dinner table with extension, a solid polished mahogany parlor set for $28, a mahogany rocker for $3.50, an oak three-drawer dresser with French beveled mirror for $7, and a mahogany music cabinet for $5.50. If you really wanted to show off and could afford (not many could), you could splurge $245 for a leather settee. And if you were well off, you could furnish your home entertainment with a Llwellyn piano for $200 and full-size oak cabinet Victrola record player for another $200.

By 1933 when production of the $10 Indian ceased, Americans had endured the first truly global armed conflict, Prohibition (repealed in 1933), the rise of the Mafia, the Crash of '29, and the Great Depression.

People sought relief from Depression drab by listening to radio for entertainment or going to the new "talkie" motion picture shows. They kept up with the times by reading Life magazine, Collier's Weekly, Reader's Digest, Ladies' Home Journal and the Saturday Evening Post featuring the popular Americana covers by illustrator

Norman Rockwell and fiction by premier writers John Steinbeck, William Saroyan, C. S. Forester, Louis L'Amour, and Ray Bradbury.

Seven presidents occupied the White House during the tenure of the $10 Indian – Theodore Roosevelt, William Howard Taft, Woodrow Wilson, Warren Harding, Calvin Coolidge, Herbert Hoover, and Franklin Roosevelt.

Nine directors presided over U.S. Mint operations during the quarter century the $10 Indian gold coin circulated – Frank Leach, A. Piatt Andrew, George Roberts, Robert Wooley, F.J.H. Engelken, Raymond Baker, F.E. Scobey, Robert Grant, and Nellie Tayloe Ross.

The age of the $10 Indian Eagle covered a time of major change in the United States and the world. America was growing up fast, no longer what we would now call "an emerging nation" but a full-fledged world power. The Industrial Revolution was already beginning to give way to The Information Age as wireless communication and new advances in electronics sped the evolution to the modern era of technology.

Political and sociological mutations were changing the geopolitical landscape. It was the sunset of the Victorian age. The communist revolution in Russia set the foundations for the coming Cold War. Adolf Hitler was sowing the seeds of World War II and the Holocaust. Women got to vote and could work outside the home; American family life changed as traditional family roles changed.

The $10 Indian Head Eagle symbolizes the early 20th century in America, marking the turning point in history when America came of age. Owning one of these coins affords the collector a tangible link to this memorable era, a physical connection to our storied past.

Covers from Collier's Weekly *and* Ladies' Home Journal, *March 1907.*

Louis E. Eliasberg
THE KING OF GOLD COINS

Louis E. Eliasberg Sr. came to be known as "The King of Coins" after he accomplished a feat many thought to be impossible: Over a period of less than two decades, from 1934 to 1950, Eliasberg assembled the only complete collection of U.S. coins – the only one that contained regular-issue coins of every denomination from every date they were issued and every mint that made them in those years. News of this achievement not only electrified fellow hobbyists, but also impressed the entire nation. It was considered so significant that Life magazine, then required reading for millions of Americans, featured Eliasberg and his coins in a lavish photo layout.

Yet, this "King of Coins" didn't have kingly wealth. He lived comfortably on his income as a Baltimore banker, but his budget for buying coins was not unlimited. Nor was he known as a big spender: Dealers who did business with him found him to be a cautious buyer who took out his checkbook only after careful deliberation.

Eliasberg wasn't even a hobbyist when he started buying coins: He did so as a way to circumvent the Gold Surrender Order of 1933, which required U.S. citizens to turn in their gold coins, but exempted collectible coins. "I realized the only way I could legally acquire gold was by becoming a numismatist," he explained years later. "So in 1934, to the extent of my means, I started buying gold coins."

Soon bitten by the hobby bug, he started buying other coins as well, and within a few years he had built a respectable collection. Then, in 1942, came a marvelous opportunity: He was able to purchase outright the outstanding collection of John H. Clapp – in the process acquiring many rare coins he didn't already possess. That's when he began thinking seriously of pursuing the impossible dream: a U.S. coin collection with "one of everything." He prepared a list of coins he lacked and started tracking them down in auctions and dealers' inventories.

"Eliasberg struck me as a gentleman," one prominent numismatist later recalled. "He was tall, aristocratic, a genius at finance, but he didn't know very much about coins … He knew more about making money." His success at making money has become the stuff of legends in the coin collecting community. During the decade and a half it took him to complete his collection, Eliasberg spent less than $400,000. When the collection was sold, at a series of auctions between 1982 and 2005, it realized a grand total of roughly $55 million – more than 100 times what he had paid.

The gold coins he started buying in 1934 not only turned Eliasberg from a numismatic novice into a great collector, but also ended up confirming his status as a very successful investor. In short, even if he had never begun pursuing the seemingly impossible dream of collecting "one of everything," Eliasberg would have made millions just through his decision to buy gold coins as collectibles.

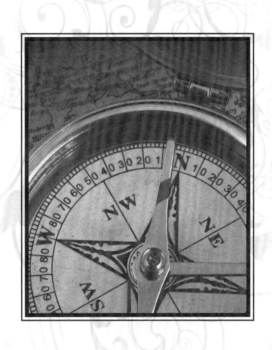

COLLECTING INDIAN HEAD $2 ½, $5 AND $10 GOLD COINS

I. Why Are These Coins So Popular?

These three Indian Head series have long been popular with collectors. There are a number of reasons for the popularity of these coins:

Beautiful Design: Their striking designs are considered to be among the most beautiful of all American coins. Simply put, people prefer to buy a coin that is universally declared beautiful, rather than one that is considered unattractive.

Affordability: They are very affordable. Many quality "uncirculated" dates can be purchased for less than $2,000, and "gem" examples of many dates can still be purchased for less than $15,000.

Value Potential: Compared to their previous market highs of 1989, they appear to be very undervalued in today's market. Remarkably, certain dates in the series are currently selling for 30 to 40 cents on the dollar versus their previous highs. For people who appreciate good "relative value", these series are irresistible.

Completability: These are three of only a handful of United States regular issue gold coin series not currently being minted that can be completed or nearly completed with moderate effort.

Uniqueness: Bela Lyon Pratt's Indian Head design, used on both Quarter Eagles and Half Eagles, is unique in the annals of American coinage. It is the only design which the devices and the lettering are "incuse" – i.e., they are sunken rather than raised. This unique design has always made the Indian Head Quarter and Half Eagle very popular with collectors.

II. How To Collect Indian Head $2 ½, $5 and $10 Gold Coins

The collector has a few interesting options when it comes to this series. Here are some suggestions on how to collect these magnificent coins.

*As A Type Coin: A "type" collection would include a single example of these designs. Due to the affordability of higher grades (in this case, "higher grade" would refer to Mint State-64 and above), it is possible to acquire an exceptional example for a reasonable price.

*By Mint: Indian Head Quarter Eagles were produced at two mints: Philadelphia and Denver. It is easy to assemble a two coin set, using one piece from each of these mints. The $5 Indian mint set would include examples from Denver, New Orleans, Philadelphia, and San Francisco. The $10 Indian would include examples from Denver, San Francisco and Philadelphia.

*By Year: Indian Head Quarter Eagles were produced during thirteen different years. A collector on a somewhat limited budget can eliminate the need for buying the expensive 1911-D (the key to the series) by using a 1911 Philadelphia as the single example of an Indian Head Quarter Eagle produced during this year. For Indian Half Eagles there are only 10 years to collect 1908-1916 and 1929. The Indian Eagles were only minted in 15 years between 1907-1933.

*By Date: Some collectors prefer to focus on one or two specific dates. They might like the 1926, as an example, because it is their birth year, or it was the year in which their parents were married. While we do not suggest trying to "corner the market" on a specific date, focusing your collecting energies on a specific issue of meaning to you can be very enjoyable.

*As A Complete Set: The most popular and recommended way to collect these series is to assemble a complete set. Typically, collectors try to assemble sets in similar grades. The most popular grades to assemble sets are Mint State-62 through Mint State-65. In Mint State-62 and Mint State-63, these sets are reasonably easy to complete. Mint State-64 is a hard set to complete. Mint State-65 is also a very hard set to complete. However, the beauty of the Indian Head Quarter Eagle series is the fact that a complete set in Mint State-65 is realistically completable. The same can not be said for some of the other major United States gold types.

*Proofs: Eight different dates of Proof Indian Head $2½, $5 and $10 gold coins were produced. Dated from 1908 through 1915, these issues are all rare. They form an interesting set as the finishes and coloration are very different on certain issues. As an example, the 1908 comes with very dark coloration and very granular matte surfaces, while the 1909 has a medium gold coloration with a totally different satin appearance to the surfaces. Proofs were minted in both matte (sandblast) and Roman (satin) finishes.

III. Buying Tips For Collectors

I have been buying Indian Head gold coins for over forty years and have purchased thousands of individual coins. I would like to share some buying tips with you that I have developed over the years. Refer to the date by date analysis for coins I identify as "keys" and "sleepers".

*Stretch For the Keys: A "key" coin is one that is considered to be a major rarity within a specific series of coins. Collectors often stretch a bit (pay more) when purchasing "key" coins.

*Identify the Sleepers: A "sleeper" coin is one that is considered to be undervalued when compared to other issues within a series. These are issues that are many times scarcer than the most available coins but for the time being sell for a relatively small premium. As the Indian series becomes more heavily collected and better researched (and the publication of this book will introduce thousands of new collectors to this area of numismatics), the opportunity to buy these sleepers at "ground floor" prices will probably end.

*Build A Set: I have long advocated the value of putting together sets of coins. For collectors, the Indian Head series are better adapted to this strategy than some other United states gold coins. The reason? Simply that these sets are relatively easy to complete, so most collectors decide to take this route. At certain times when nicely matched complete sets are offered for sale at coin shows or at auctions, dealers and collectors have paid notable premiums to acquire them. When you go to sell your Indian Head gold coins, having a nicely matched complete set should make them more marketable, and should enable you to maximize the value of each coin you own.

*Read This Book: A considerable amount of knowledge went into the writing of this book. Don't just let it sit on your desk. If you are purchasing coins worth thousands of dollars, you owe it to yourself to become familiar with these series. Study this book and carefully read each date entry each time you are considering adding a coin to your set. This book has enough important information inside that it will help you to assemble a truly great set of coins.

HOW TO PROTECT YOUR GOLD COINS FROM THEFT

I advise coin collectors to store their most valuable rare coins in a safe deposit box at a bank or security center and then "don't be predictable when going there." Bear in mind that professional coin dealers do the same thing as part of their regular business practice, especially with their more valuable rare coins, or with gold and platinum bullion coins.

I would specifically warn collectors and business owners who live in hurricane-prone areas to use safety deposit boxes for their most valuable coins. Just ask the victims of Hurricane Ike, which hit Texas in 2008, leaving hundreds of houses and their contents open to looters, or destroyed.

If you are going to keep rare coins or bullion at home to enjoy, which is understandable, here are some helpful tips to reduce the chances they will be stolen.

(1) Buy a safe that is too heavy for thieves to easily carry off. Secure it to the floor if possible. Time is your friend in a robbery.

(2) Make sure your safe offers adequate protection from fire, too.

(3) Be careful about who you tell about your collection and its value.

(4) Check your coin insurance coverage with your homeowner's policy. Make sure it covers collectable value. List and photograph your most valuable coins for insurance purposes.

(5) Don't leave your collection out so children, maids or workers can see them and access them. Many a rare coin has ended up in vending machines thanks to son's or daughter's needs and ignorance.

To further deter robberies:

(6) Get to know your neighbors well and watch out for each other. Have the Post Office hold your mail while you are out of town; and have coin-related material sent to a post office box.

(7) Don't let newspapers pile up, or snow remain undisturbed in winter, or your yard unmowed in summer, or leave advertisement hangers on door knobs.

(8) Keep your doors and windows locked and routinely check them again. A common burglar may enter through an unlocked garage door or back door.

(9) Make sure your locks, doors and frames are well made and solid.

(10) Don't leave boxes from expensive purchases in the yard for pickup.

(11) Don't announce vacations on Facebook, MySpace, or any other public forum.

(12) Don't have your alarm control where it is easily visible to see if it's set.

(13) A loud television or radio can be an effective deterrent if left on.

(14) Loud dogs also deter thieves.

(15) Don't store your coins in your bedroom or medicine cabinet as thieves usually go there first.

CERTIFIED GRADES ASSIGNED

Certified grades assigned to collectible coins range from poor (1) to perfect (70), with plus (+) grades in between some grades. A coin can either be designated mint state (struck for circulation) or proof (usually specially struck for collectors). The following are some of the grades you may see on a certified coin and a brief description of what it means.

GRADE	ADJECTIVE	DESCRIPTION
P-1	Poor	All designs are barely recognizable
AG-3	About Good	Very heavily worn but part of date may be readable
G-4	Good	All design elements are visible but may be faint
VG-8	Very Good	Well worn but all design elements clear although flat
F-12	Fine	Even moderate wear so that entire design is bold
VF-20	Very Fine	Moderate wear on high points of design but all major details clear. A pleasing circulated coin.
VF-30	Choice Very Fine	A very fine example just short of the next grade with minimum contact marks or other imperfections
XF EF 40	Extremely Fine	Design is lightly worn with most high points visible with slight wear or flatness. Luster may be present in protected areas
XF-45	Choice Extremely Fine	A bit more luster or less contact marks than previous grade
AU-50	Almost Uncirculated	Traces of light wear on most high points. Usually 25-50 percent of mint luster evident
AU-53	Choice Almost Uncirculated	Same as above but fewer contact marks or other imperfections
AU-55	Premium Almost Uncirculated	At least 50 percent of luster evident and less contact marks or other imperfections
AU-58	Premium Almost Uncirculated	At least 75 percent or more luster present and less imperfections

UNCIRCULATED GRADES

GRADE	ADJECTIVE	DESCRIPTION
MS-60	Uncirculated	No wear but may show considerable bag marks, discoloration, abrasion, detail weakness and other unsightly traits including diminished luster. Out of an original bag of coins the most imperfect coins are the MS-60s. In some early series, for example 18th and 19th century coinage, where mint state examples are rare, MS-60s are coveted. In most 20th century series MS-60s are considered too low a grade for rare coin investors to consider for most dates.
MS-61	Uncirculated	Less imperfections than MS-60s
MS-62	Choice Uncirculated	Lighter marks and abrasion and 90-100 percent full luster. The first really choice mint state grade. May have some strike weakness.
MS-63	Choice Uncirculated	A pleasing uncirculated coin with full luster. Most contact marks are on the periphery. Contact marks may be present in key central areas but are scattered. Strike may be a trifle less than full. Other minor imperfections may be present.
MS-64	Gem Uncirculated	Less marks in key central areas, full luster, almost full detail and good overall eye appeal separate this grade from lower grades.
MS-65	Gem Uncirculated	Only a few marks in key central areas and minor marks on the periphery. Excellent eye appeal whether the coin is brilliant or has attractive coloration (toning). Details are strong and mint made imperfections, if any, are barely noticeable.
MS-66	Gem Uncirculated	Slightly more eye appealing than MS-65. Contact marks or frost breaks are slight.
MS-67	Superb Uncirculated	All imperfections require intense scrutiny to locate. This is a mind boggling eye-appealing specimen.
MS-68	Superb Uncirculated	An amazing coin that experts often use a term like wonder coin to describe its eye appeal and immaculate surfaces.
MS-69	Superb Uncirculated	Only under intense magnification can any undesirable trait be discerned. Phenomenal eye appeal.
MS-70	Perfect Uncirculated	Almost nonexistent.

Accurate determination of these grades can only be done through extensive comparisons to standard grading service grading sets.

7 DIFFERENT

PLACES TO QUICKLY SELL YOUR GOLD COINS AND JEWELRY

Why has a rise in gold prices also led to a universal rise in consumer complaints and potential coin lawsuits aimed at some gold coin and jewelry buyers?

Recent testing done by Consumer Reports, ABC's Good Morning America and regional award winning weekly The Examiner provide some answers. I will address seven different business models and will briefly summarize their advantages and disadvantages. They are listed in order of who often pays the most to who often pays the least.

1. LARGE NATIONAL COIN DEALER

ADVANTAGES – Typically pay the most for types of gold coins or jewelry they specialize in and they are usually reputable nationally and locally but you must verify this. The Examiner story found surveyed major reputable national coin dealers paid as much as 4-5 times what some hotel coin buyers paid on some rare gold coins. Are usually the quickest in and out to deal with.

DISADVANTAGES – May be far away from where you are and may not buy jewelry. You still must check out their reputation and if they are Better Business Bureau accredited.

2. LOCAL COIN DEALER

ADVANTAGES – They are in your area and The Examiner story found they often paid 3-4 times what hotel coin buyers paid for the same gold coins. If they routinely deal in gold jewelry they may make some of the highest offers for old gold jewelry. They are usually quick to deal with. They may buy bulk groups of lower value collector coins that don't interest some national coin dealers.

DISADVANTAGES – Even if reputable and knowledgeable they may pay 10-20% less than major dealers for rare coins and gold jewelry. Some local coin dealers are not Better Business Bureau accredited and may offer much less due to lack of expertise or integrity. Check out their reputation carefully.

3. JEWELRY SHOPS

ADVANTAGES – For jewelry, not rare gold coins, may be very competitive with local or national coin shop if reputable and Better Business Bureau accredited. Finely crafted jewelry can bring premiums.

DISADVANTAGES - Experts for buying jewelry may not always be on premises and you must make sure of local reputation and if they are Better Business Bureau accredited. Often may pay melt value or slightly higher for rare gold coins that are worth multiples of melt value.

4. PAWN SHOPS

ADVANTAGES – You can buy back some products you sell if you want and some are BBB accredited and give you very competitive prices locally on gold bullion and jewelry.

DISADVANTAGES – Often not in best part of town, bars and barbed wire, and may offer less than previous three. Rare gold coins are usually not their specialty, thus their rare gold coin offers are usually not competitive. Check out their reputation carefully.

5. GOLD PARTIES

ADVANTAGES – You know the person holding the party and it's held in a comfortable setting.

DISADVANTAGES – Prices paid are often far less than the first three and you often don't know as much about the actual buyers' knowledge and integrity and if they are Better Business Bureau accredited. The host typically makes 10% too!

6. HOTEL BUYERS

ADVANTAGES – They're in your locale and you get paid immediately.

DISADVANTAGES – May pay as little as 20¢ on the dollar compared to buyers previously listed #1 and #2 and they may not really know what they are looking at. They also may not give you an itemized receipt and the process can take the longest. One common coin may take 45 minutes to get a value. Some have been the subject of numerous customer complaints. They may not be Better Business Bureau accredited.

7. MAIL-AWAY GOLD BUYERS

ADVANTAGES – No in person contact and fairly simple to send.

DISADVANTAGES – Offers may be about 20¢ on the dollar and you may have to negotiate to get that or higher. Some customers have reported having their gold items lost or melted and could not be returned and were refused reimbursement. Some companies have been the subject of numerous customer complaints resulting in new laws to address some business practices. They may not be Better Business Bureau accredited.

In conclusion, I would advise getting an opinion from a reputable coin dealer before selling your gold coins or jewelry by mail or to a transient buyer at a gold party or hotel. Always get an offer from the dealer that originally sold you the coins.

DATE BY DATE ANALYSIS

This date by date analysis of the Indian Head Quarter Eagles series goes over many topics of interest to the collector that includes a general description or history of each piece, along with comments on each issue's characteristics of strike, luster, color, and eye appeal.

Each issue includes a ranking of Overall Rarity and Uncirculated Rarity. Overall Rarity is determined by my estimate of the total number of coins that exist in all grades. Uncirculated Rarity is determined by the total number of coins that exist in MS62 - MS65 grades tabulated by total population figures supplied by PCGS and NGC.

You will find that there is no price listed under each coin as pricing information becomes dated relatively quickly. You should speak to your dealer or representative for current pricing on the coin(s) you are interested in.

Counterfeit gold coins imported from China are a growing concern to the numismatic community. Replicas are sometimes seen listed without proper identification on various online auction sites and at flea markets. Only buy Indian Gold coins from a reputable dealer and preferably authenticated and graded by either PCGS or NGC.

Specifications

$2½ INDIAN HEAD QUARTER EAGLES

Designer: Bela Lyon Pratt

Minted From: 1908-1915 & 1925-1929

Minted At: Philadelphia & Denver

Diameter: 18 millimeters

Composition: .900 gold, .100 copper

Weight: 4.18 grams

Net Weight: .12094 ounce pure gold

Edge: Reeded to prevent gold shaving

SYMBOLOGY

1 Inscribed around the top rim of the obverse is the word LIBERTY.

2 The obverse features the first realistic depiction of a Native American Chief in war bonnet ever used on a U.S. gold coin. Like the other devices on the coin, the Indian figure is incuse, meaning sunken rather than raised.

3 The obverse features THIRTEEN STARS representing the original colonies, which are divided by the LIBERTY device at the top rim.

4 The initials BLP of designer Bela Lyon Pratt.

5 The mint year date runs along the obverse's center bottom rim.

6 "UNITED STATES OF AMERICA" is inscribed around the top rim of the coin's reverse denoting the coin as US legal tender.

7 The motto "IN GOD WE TRUST" is inscribed near the right rim of the reverse just to the right of the eagle's back.

8 The central device on the reverse is a majestic eagle, which has traditionally been symbolic for the freedom represented by America.

9 The motto "E PLURIBUS UNUM", which is Latin for "out of many, one," is inscribed on the reverse just to the left of the eagle's breast.

10 The mint mark location is just to the left of the arrow tips. On the pictured coin, there is no mint mark, which indicates this coin was minted at Philadelphia.

11 The eagle sits atop a bundle of arrows around which is wrapped an olive branch. Together, these two symbolize America's military strength and readiness to defend its interests and its desire for peace.

12 The legal tender denomination of "2 1/2 DOLLARS" is inscribed along the bottom rim of the coin's reverse.

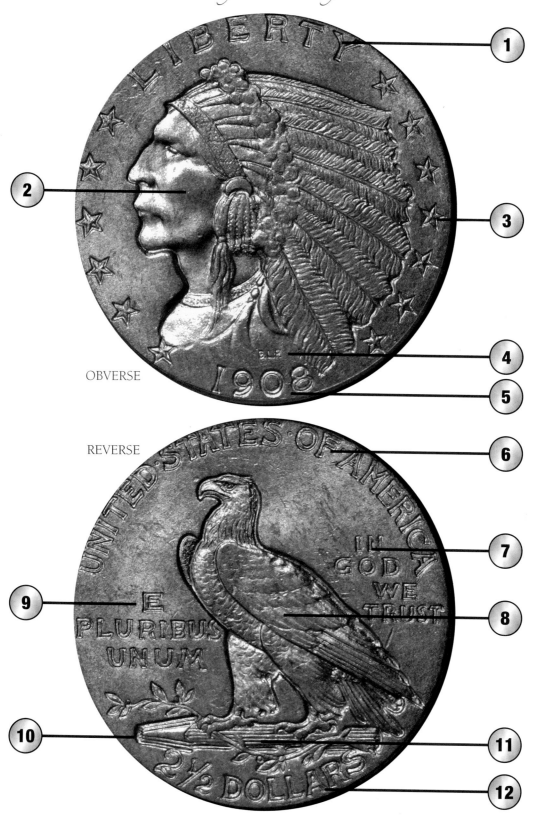

OBVERSE

REVERSE

1908

Business Strike

Proof

———

The 1908 is a popular issue due to its status as the first Indian Head Quarter Eagle. As with many 20th century first-year-of-issue pieces, it was saved as a curiosity and more exist in higher grades than is generally believed. But the demand level for this date remains very high and gems are eagerly sought-after by collectors.

———

Mintage: **564,821 + 236 Proofs**

Overall Rarity: 6 of 15

Uncirculated Rarity:

    MS-62   6 of 15
    MS-63   9 of 15
    MS-64   10 of 15
    MS-65   13 of 15

The obverse is generally among the better struck issues of this type with very strong detail noted on the Indian's feathers and headband. The reverse, however, always shows weakness on the eagle's wing. This is actually not due to strike, but because of a lack of detail on the die. This problem was corrected on later issues, but on the 1908, it means that many coins with reverse weakness are mistaken for worn pieces.

Most show marks on the surfaces that range from slight to severe. There are some pieces that were probably put away in 1908 and have been carefully preserved since. It is possible for the collector to locate a piece that has above-average surfaces.

The luster seen on this issue is not as good as that found on the later Philadelphia dates. It is most often found with a soft, slightly satiny texture that is appealing, but not as "flashy" as, say, on the 1925 through 1929 dates.

The coloration seen on original specimens is usually a medium to deep green-gold hue. Specimens with attractive color are relatively easy to find.

The overall level of eye appeal is slightly below average, primarily due to the weakness on the eagle's wing mentioned above. In addition, some 1908 Quarter Eagles are dull and have a somewhat grainy appearance. However, it is definitely possible to locate a piece that is cosmetically appealing.

To qualify in the Condition Census, a 1908 Indian Head Quarter Eagle must grade Mint State-66.

1908 Indian Quarter Eagles were struck with a dark matte finish and are found with deep olive-gold coloration. It is believed that around half of the original mintage figure of 236 pieces exist today. The 1908 is the most available Proof Indian Head Quarter Eagle in high grades and most survivors are in the Proof-64 to Proof-65 range. As with circulation strikes for this year, the Proofs appear to be saved as novelties by both collectors and non-collectors. For the collector who is seeking a single Proof issue of this design, the 1908 is an excellent choice.

1909

Business Strike

Proof

The 1909 is very similar in overall rarity to the 1910, but it is slightly more available in higher grades. It is considerably rarer than the 1908 in high grades, and many times rarer than the 1926-1928 Philadelphia issues in Mint State-65.

Mintage: **441,760 + 139 Proofs**

Overall Rarity: 2 of 15

Uncirculated Rarity:

MS-62	2 of 15
MS-63	4 of 15
MS-64	5 of 15
MS-65	10 of 15

The obverse is sharply struck although not quite as much as on the 1908 Quarter Eagles. There is sometimes weakness on the center of the obverse and on the tips of the feathers to the right of the date. The reverse die problems that existed in 1908 were solved in 1909 and the wing feathers are generally well struck and show definition.

Most 1909 Quarter Eagles display noticeable marks on the surfaces. It is not uncommon for examples to have mint-made spots. These are not considered detracting unless they are extensive or situated in obvious locations. For some reason, many 1909 Quarter Eagles show scratches in the fields. When buying a high grade example, make certain that it does not have detracting scratches.

The luster is among the best seen on the early dates of this series. Some pieces are very frosty while others have luster that is a blend of reflectiveness and satiny texture and resembles that seen on Proofs of this year.

The natural coloration for 1909 Quarter Eagles is light to medium yellow-gold. Some show green-gold or light rose toning. It is becoming quite hard to find a 1909 Quarter Eagle that has original color and such pieces are beginning to sell for premiums to knowledgeable collectors.

The overall level of eye appeal ranges from slightly below average to average. Most are reasonably well struck, but show numerous marks on the surfaces and have inferior luster. Pieces are sometimes available with good eye appeal and the collector should wait for one, which qualifies as such.

To qualify in the Condition Census, a 1909 Indian Head Quarter Eagle must grade Mint State-66.

Most 1909 Proof Indian Head Quarter Eagles were struck with a light satiny finish that is known to collectors as "Roman Gold." The coloration of these Proofs is a rich yellow-gold and the texture is a hybrid of matte and mirror surfaces. 139 were struck and approximately 55-65 are known. This is the rarest Proof Indian Head Quarter Eagle in high grades and Gems are extremely rare.

1910

Business Strike

Proof

The 1910 is very similar in overall rarity to the 1909, but it is slightly less available in higher grades. It is considerably rarer than the 1908 in high grades and many times rarer than the 1926-1928 Philadelphia issues in Mint State-65.

Mintage: **492,000 + 682* Proofs**

Overall Rarity: 4 of 15

Uncirculated Rarity:

MS-62	5 of 15
MS-63	5 of 15
MS-64	4 of 15
MS-65	7 of 15

This is one of the best struck early date Indian Head Quarter Eagles. On the obverse, the only area that is not generally well detailed is the part of the headdress covering the Indian's ear. The eagle's wing feathers are sharp and the breast feathers are often fully detailed. On some 1910 Quarter Eagles, there is some swelling of the die noted that is probably the result of die buckling. This does not affect the value.

The 1910 Quarter Eagle is a very hard issue to locate without abrasions. In addition, many are seen with mint-made spots or small planchet problems. It is very hard to locate a coin that has clean, undisturbed surfaces and such pieces appear to be significantly undervalued in today's market.

The luster is considerably better on this issue than it is on the 1908 and the 1909. It is frosty in texture with some areas of satiny surfaces mixed into the reverse fields.

The natural coloration is a medium to deep yellow gold shades. Less often, 1910 Quarter Eagles have orange-gold color.

The overall level of eye appeal seen on the 1910 Quarter Eagle is below average. While most are well struck, it is very hard to find a piece that is not severely abraded and, which does not have impaired luster.

To qualify for the Condition Census, a 1910 Indian Head Quarter Eagle must grade Mint State-66.

*The mintage figure for Proof 1910 Quarter Eagles is listed as 682 pieces, but this is almost certainly incorrect. Based on the number known to exist, it is much more likely that the original mintage figure was somewhere in the area of 175 to 200. Of these, an estimated 75 to 90 coins exist today. The coloration is similar to that seen on the 1909 proofs with a distinctive yellow-gold appearance and the so-called Roman Gold finish. Proofs are usually seen in the Proof-63 to Proof-64 range and Gem examples are quite rare..

Business Strike

Proof

1911

The 1911 has the second highest mintage of any date in this series. It is the most common date from the 1910's in terms of its overall rarity, (i.e., the total number known to exist) but it is a very rare coin in the higher Uncirculated grades; nearly comparable to such better known issues as the 1912 and the 1913.

Mintage: 704,000 **+ 191 Proofs**

Overall Rarity: 10 of 15

Uncirculated Rarity:

MS-62	10 of 15
MS-63	10 of 15
MS-64	8 of 15
MS-65	6 of 15

The obverse strike is sometimes reasonably sharp, but more often than not there is weakness on the three lower feathers, parts of the headdress and on the brow. The reverse is not quite as sharp as on the 1909 and 1910 issues and some coins are not fully detailed on the eagle's breast and the upper portion of the wing, near the neck. Any coin that is sharply struck on the obverse and reverse should sell for a premium.

The 1911 is a very scarce coin in the higher Mint State grades. This is due to the fact that most have numerous small marks on the surfaces. It is not uncommon to see pieces with mint-made copper spots as well.

The luster is below average. It is most often very grainy in texture. Any example that has appealing, undisturbed luster is extremely scarce and in great demand among date collectors.

The coloration is frequently a medium to deep greenish-gold with some orange-hues mixed in. A small number of 1911 Quarter Eagles show natural light yellow-gold color and this appearance tends to be considerably more attractive than the look mentioned above.

The 1911 Quarter Eagle is a very hard date to locate with good eye appeal. Many are not well struck and most show obvious marks on the surfaces. The luster is often not very good and the natural coloration is generally not viewed as attractive by people unfamiliar with this series. A 1911 Quarter Eagle with good eye appeal is a hard issue to locate and such pieces are extremely popular.

To qualify for the Condition Census, a 1911 Indian Head Quarter Eagle must grade Mint State-66.

There were 191 Proof 1911 Quarter Eagles struck. An estimated 85-95 are known today. The typical survivor tends to be considerably nicer than other Proofs of this type and some truly superb pieces are known. In fact, a great majority of the ultra high grade Proof Indian Quarter Eagles that exist (i.e., in Proof-67) are dated 1911. Proofs from this year have a very dark olive coloration that is similar in hue to the 1908. The dark matte finish has a highly granular texture that is different than that seen on the 1908 and is really not similar to that found on any other Proof issue of this design.

1911-D

The 1911-D is the rarest Indian Head Quarter Eagle in all grades combined. There are a number of other factors that make this the most desirable single coin in the Indian Head Quarter Eagle set. It has the lowest mintage by a huge margin and is the only issue whose mintage is below 100,000. It is the first Indian Head Quarter Eagle to be produced at a mint other than Philadelphia and one of just three non-Philadelphia issues of this design. Collectors of this era usually didn't pay attention to mint marked thus many were not saved.

Mintage: **55,680**

Overall Rarity: 1 of 15

Uncirculated Rarity:

MS-62   1 of 15
MS-63   1 of 15
MS-64   2 of 15
MS-65   3 of 15

The quality of strike seen on the 1911-D is better than generally believed. The obverse detail is nearly always sharp although some may have minor weakness in the center. The reverse shows good definition, including the center. All genuine 1911-D Quarter Eagles have a raised wire rim on the obverse from approximately 1:00 to 5:00. This can be seen even on very low grade coins and serves as an immediate hallmark of identification.

Some 1911-D Quarter Eagles have an extremely weak mintmark. On a few, the mintmark is so weak that it is nearly impossible to see with the naked eye. These are sometimes designated as "Weak D" coins by PCGS and NGC. It is our opinion that collectors should avoid 1911-D Weak D Quarter Eagles as it makes no sense to pay a strong premium for a mintmarked issue and to not be able to clearly see the mintmark.

Many 1911-D Quarter Eagles have small to medium-sized mint-made copper spots; these seem to be more noticeable on the reverse than the obverse. Most have noticeable abrasions as well.

The luster is a combination of granular and frosty, which produces a sort of texture that is unique to this issue. Most knowledgeable numismatists can easily recognize this date because of its unique luster. The quality of the luster is slightly below average and the typical 1911-D Quarter Eagle has a somewhat subdued appearance. A few are known with very good frosty luster and these are both rare and desirable.

The 1911-D Quarter Eagle is most often seen with medium to deep orange-gold coloration. A few are also known that show a more sedate medium green-gold hue. It has become very hard to locate an example that has original color as many have been cleaned, dipped or enhanced in recent years.

The quality of eye appeal seen on the 1911-D Quarter Eagle varies greatly. There are some very handsome coins known in all grade ranges, but most collectors wind-up with an example that is very low-end for the grade. It is our strong belief that since this is the key issue in the Indian Head Quarter Eagle set the collector should stretch and try to buy the nicest example that is feasible. An otherwise unexceptional set can be made very desirable with the addition of a very nice 1911-D.

To qualify for the Condition Census, a 1911-D Indian Head Quarter Eagle must grade Mint State-66. A very high end Mint State-65 piece may qualify as well.

Business Strike

Proof

1912

The 1912 is one of the scarcest Philadelphia Indian Head Quarter Eagles and it is among the rarest dates in the entire series in the higher Uncirculated grades. For the collector putting together a very high quality set, the 1912 is always a true "stopper."

Mintage: **616,000 + 197 Proofs**

Overall Rarity: **5 of 15**

Uncirculated Rarity:

MS-62	4 of 15
MS-63	3 of 15
MS-64	3 of 15
MS-65	4 of 15

Most 1912 Quarter Eagles show a good overall quality of strike. On the obverse, there may be some weakness at the center, but it is possible to locate a piece with almost complete definition on the feathers. The reverse is nearly always boldly struck with very sharp detail on the wings and breast. On late strikes, there may be some weakness at the borders and the tips of the stars may appear to flow into the rim.

The surfaces are usually noticeably abraded and many show mint-made spotting. A 1912 Quarter Eagle that is very clean is quite hard to locate. The reverse field above the motto is sometimes very granular; this is also mint-made and is not considered detracting.

This date is known for having a peculiar granular luster that tends not to be especially "flashy." With lackluster coins being the norm, any piece that has vibrant luster is considered highly desirable.

The natural coloration ranges from medium orange-gold to green-gold and even a light to medium yellow-gold. It is hard to locate a 1912 Quarter Eagle that still has its full original color intact.

The eye appeal for this date is generally below average. Most 1912 Quarter Eagles are well struck, but they have overly abraded surfaces and inferior luster. Examples that have good eye appeal are scarce and in strong demand among serious collectors of this series.

To qualify for the Condition Census, a 1912 Indian Head Quarter Eagle grades Mint State-66. A very high end Mint State-65 piece may qualify as well.

197 Proofs were struck. The survival rate appears to be lower than for other Proofs of this design and there are approximately 55-65 known. The coins that exist tend to be extremely high quality and the collector is more likely to be offered a Proof-65 or Proof-66 1912 Quarter Eagle than a Proof-63 or a Proof-64. The finish used this year is a fine sandblast texture, which is different than that found on either the 1908 or the 1911. The color is a medium green-gold with some yellowish-gold color noted within the surfaces.

1913

Business Strike

Proof

Because it has the highest mintage figure of any date in this series, the 1913 is not especially difficult to locate in the lower Uncirculated grades. However, it becomes very scarce in Mint State-64 and it is quite rare in Mint State-65.

Mintage: **722,000 + 165 Proofs**

Overall Rarity: **9 of 15**

Uncirculated Rarity:

MS-62   9 of 15
MS-62   8 of 15
MS-64   7 of 15
MS-65   5 of 15

The 1913 Quarter Eagle is generally seen with a very sharp strike. On most examples, the obverse is nearly fully detailed with the exception of some of the feathers at the center, which may show weakness. The reverse is well detailed with sharp breast and eagle feathers.

Most have noticeably abraded surfaces with deep, detracting marks visible in the fields. A number show mint-made spots as well. It is extremely challenging to locate a 1913 Quarter Eagle with clean surfaces, but they do exist.

There are two types of luster seen on this issue. The majority of coins have a fairly granular texture that tends to be a bit dull. A small number have more attractive frosty luster. While this is more aesthetically appealing, it is also quite hard to find pieces that have this sort of texture and they generally command premium prices.

The natural coloration seen on 1913 Quarter Eagles is most often a medium to deep yellow-gold hue, which can be especially attractive. This is becoming a very hard date to find with natural coloration.

The overall level of eye appeal is slightly below average. The typical 1913 Quarter Eagle is well detailed, but has heavy abrasions and poor luster. There are some extremely nice pieces known, however, and these are always in great demand among specialists.

To qualify for the Condition Census, a 1913 Indian Head Quarter Eagle must grade Mint State-66. A very high end Mint State-65 piece may qualify as well.

165 Proofs were produced. The survival rate is very similar to the 1912 and the same approximate number of survivors, in the area of 55 to 65 pieces, are estimated to exist. Interestingly, a very high number of these are extremely well-preserved with more Proof-65 and Proof-66 pieces being known than those in the Proof-63 to Proof-64 range. The Proofs of this year have a fine sandblast finish that is very similar in appearance to that seen on the 1912. The coloration is somewhat different with the typical hue being a bit more golden-green than on the 1912's.

Business Strike

Proof

1914

The mintage figure dropped significantly in 1914 with nearly a half million fewer Quarter Eagles produced at the Philadelphia Mint than in the previous year. The 1914 is the second rarest Indian Head Quarter Eagles in terms of its overall rarity and it is one of the rarest in high grades. Gem examples are very rare.

Mintage: **240,000 + 117 Proofs**

Overall Rarity: 3 of 15

Uncirculated Rarity:

MS-62   3 of 15
MS-63   2 of 15
MS-64   1 of 15
MS-65   2 of 15

Both the obverse and the reverse show very sharp detail with almost complete definition in the centers. There is sometimes weakness at the central obverse behind the ear of the Indian, but this tends to be unobtrusive. Many 1914 Quarter Eagles show buckling of the dies at the borders and this produces a somewhat "swelled" appearance. This does not affect a coin's grade or value.

This issue is characterized by heavily abraded surfaces. The 1914 is among the hardest Indian Head Quarter Eagles to find with clean surfaces and many also show mint-made spots or patches of granularity.

The luster is subdued and below average in relation to other dates in this series. It usually has a decidedly granular appearance. This is further compounded by the fact that many have been cleaned or dipped. This is probably the hardest Indian Head Quarter Eagle to find with good luster.

The natural coloration that is most often seen on 1914 Quarter Eagles is a medium to deep yellow-gold. Some uncleaned pieces may exhibit attractive greenish hues as well. This is an extremely hard issue to find with original color and a number of coins that have not been cleaned or dipped do not display especially pleasing hues.

The level of eye appeal is below average. While most 1914 Quarter Eagles are very well struck, most have inferior luster and noticeably abraded surfaces. Any piece that has good eye appeal is very scarce and is eagerly sought by serious collectors of this series.

To qualify for the Condition Census, a 1914 Indian Head Quarter Eagle must grade Mint State-65.

117 Proofs were struck in 1914. This is the second lowest mintage figure for the Indian Head Quarter Eagle design. The survival rate is higher than for the 1912-1913 issues and an estimated 60-70 are known. Unlike the 1913, the 1914 is not often found in Proof-65 and higher grades. Most Proofs are in the Proof-63 to Proof-64 range and gems are very rare. The texture is a fine sandblast finish that is found only on this year and the 1915. The coloration is a dark green hue that is a shade lighter than that seen on the 1915 Proofs.

1914-D

The 1914-D is an issue whose true rarity was not understood until a few years ago. Many casual observers still feel that this is not a rare coin, but it is actually the third rarest Indian Head Quarter Eagle in terms of its overall rarity and one of the true rarities in this series in the higher Uncirculated grades.

Mintage: **448,000**

Overall Rarity: **7 of 15**

Uncirculated Rarity:

MS-62	8 of 15
MS-63	6 of 15
MS-64	6 of 15
MS-65	1 of 15

The 1914-D is not nearly as well struck as the 1911-D and it may well be the worst struck Indian Head Quarter Eagle. On the obverse, the center is often weak and the border may have a slightly buckled appearance. The reverse is much more weakly struck and most examples show considerable weakness on the eagle's leg and wing. The breast feathers are often weak as well. The mintmark is usually weak at the top, but sharper at its bottom.

Many 1914-D Quarter Eagles have numerous marks on the surfaces. There are many that also show mint-made spots. It is very hard to locate a piece that has clean surfaces and this is one of the major reasons why the grading services have encapsulated so few coins in the higher Mint State grades.

This issue has much better luster than its similarly dated Philadelphia counterpart. It has a frosty texture with some slight graininess located around the devices. On a number of pieces, the luster has impaired from mishandling or numismatic abuse.

A rather broad range of coloration has been seen on this issue. Some 1914-D Quarter Eagles have medium to deep yellow-gold color while others are a darker green-gold hue. Many of the nicest pieces known have very attractive medium to deep coppery-gold color and advanced collectors prefer this look to the other two described above.

The eye appeal for the 1914-D ranges from below average to average. Most are not well struck and show numerous abrasions on the surfaces. However, many have very good luster and color. It is not really all that hard to find an attractive 1914-D in the Mint State-63 to Mint State-64 range, but true Gems are extremely scarce and this will prove to be one of the hardest dates in the series for the connoisseur.

To qualify for the Condition Census, a 1914-D Indian Head Quarter Eagle must be Mint State-65.

1915

Business Strike

Proof

The 1915 is the final Indian Head Eagle produced during the 1910's and production of the denomination at the Philadelphia Mint was discontinued until 1926. It is a fairly common date that is well-regarded for its aesthetic appeal and popular with type collectors.

Mintage: **606,000 + 100 Proofs**

Overall Rarity: **8 of 15**

Uncirculated Rarity:

MS-62	7 of 15
MS-63	7 of 15
MS-64	9 of 15
MS-65	8 of 15

The 1915 Quarter Eagle is a well struck issue. The obverse is quite well detailed with the exception of a few of the feathers at the center, which may sometimes show slight weakness. The reverse is quite sharp with bold feathers on the eagle's wing and breasts.

The surfaces tend to be cleaner than on the 1912-1914 Philadelphia Quarter Eagles. Most are abraded and may show scratches in the fields. But there are some very clean pieces known and the collector, if he is patient, should be able to locate a 1915 Quarter Eagle that has reasonably choice surfaces.

There are two distinct types of luster seen on this date. The majority of coins have the dull, slightly grainy texture that is seen on most of the 1909-1914 Philadelphia issues. A smaller number (around 10-15%) have excellent luster that is more frosty in texture. An example with this frosty luster is considered far more desirable by collectors.

The natural coloration is a medium to deep yellow-gold with some greenish highlights. A few show a deeper coppery-orange hue. It is still possible to locate a 1915 with nice original color, but such coins are becoming more difficult to find with the passing of every year.

The eye appeal is usually average to slightly above average. Most are well struck and have fairly clean surfaces. Some show good luster and color as well. But, there are only a small handful of superb pieces known to exist and most of these are in lightly-held private collections.

To qualify for the Condition Census, a 1915 Indian Head Quarter Eagle must be Mint State-65.

Only 100 Proof 1915 Quarter Eagles were produced. This is the rarest Proof Indian Head Quarter Eagle in terms of overall rarity. There an estimated 35-45 pieces known. Survivors are usually in the Proof-63 to Proof-64 range and Gems are very rare. In fact, this is the second rarest Proof issue in high grades, trailing only the 1909. The surface texture and appearance are very similar to the 1914 and the coloration is similar as well.

1925-D

The Indian Head Quarter Eagle was not struck from 1916 to 1924. During this era, production of all gold denominations other than double eagles was non-existent (except for 1916-S Half Eagle and Eagle) as it was decided to focus gold coinage efforts on the largest denomination.

The 1925-D is significant as the only mintmarked issue of this type produced in the 1920's. It is probably the most common date in terms of overall rarity and it is the most common in high grades as well.

Mintage: 578,000

Overall Rarity: 15 of 15

Uncirculated Rarity:

MS-62	14 of 15
MS-63	14 of 15
MS-64	14 of 15
MS-65	15 of 15

Most 1925-D Quarter Eagles are poorly struck at the borders with clear signs of the dies having been buckled. The centers have some weakness as well with incomplete feather detail on the bonnet and some weakness on the eagle's breast feathers. On a number of pieces, the mintmark either appears as a blob or is very weak. There are also a few on, which the mintmark is so weak that it is nearly invisible. Some well struck 1925-D Quarter Eagles do exist and the collector should wait for one with above-average detail as it will probably become available.

Most examples have scattered marks on the surfaces and it is very hard to find a 1925-D that has clean fields. A number show mint-made copper spots, but these are not detracting unless they are extensive or situated in obvious locations.

This issue has much better luster than the two other Indian Head Quarter Eagles produced at the Denver Mint. It has a frosty texture that can be very attractive on higher grade pieces.

The coloration on high grade, original 1925-D Quarter Eagles is generally excellent. The hues seen most often are coppery-gold, rose-gold and deep yellow-gold. It is still possible to find a piece with good color without a huge effort.

The level of eye appeal for the 1925-D varies greatly. Most do not show an especially good strike, but this is compensated for by nice color and luster. If the collector is patient, he should be able to locate a 1925-D Quarter Eagle that is attractive.

To qualify for the Condition Census, a 1925-D Indian Head Quarter Eagle must be Mint State-66.

1926

The 1926 is the first Indian Head Quarter Eagle to be produced at the Philadelphia Mint since 1915. It begins a run of four issues that are regarded as the most common dates of this type.

Mintage: 446,000

Overall Rarity: 13 of 15

Uncirculated Rarity:

MS-62   13 of 15
MS-63   13 of 15
MS-64   15 of 15
MS-65   14 of 15

There are not many Indian Head Quarter Eagles that are as well struck as the 1926. The typical example has very sharp detail on the obverse with nearly full feathers. While a few are seen with some peripheral weakness due to die buckling, most are sharp in this area as well. The reverse is also sharp with nearly full feather detail on the wings, breast and inner leg of the eagle.

This is the most available Indian Head Quarter Eagle in Mint State-65 and, as a result, it is possible to locate a piece that has reasonably clean surfaces. The typical coin does show scattered small marks, but there are a number that are very clean.

The luster on this issue is excellent with a frosty texture that is quite possibly the best on any date of this type. High grade examples often have such good luster that they make ideal type pieces to illustrate the beauty of the Indian Head design.

Original pieces have a number of possible color variations. Some are known with medium green-gold hues while others are a lighter rose-gold. A smaller number exist with very attractive orange-gold. Locating one with good color remains relatively easy.

There are many truly attractive 1926 Quarter Eagles known. Most high grade pieces are well struck, have choice surfaces and excellent luster and display good color.

To qualify for the Condition Census, a 1926 Indian Head Quarter Eagle must be Mint State-66.

1927

The 1927 has the lowest mintage figure of the 1926-1929 Quarter Eagles and this makes it the least available in terms of the total number known. However, it is available in any Mint State grade up to and including Mint State-64. Gems are somewhat scarce, but are more obtainable than pre-1925 issue with the exception of the 1908.

Mintage: **388,000**

Overall Rarity: 11 of 15

Uncirculated Rarity:

MS-62	11 of 15
MS-63	11 of 15
MS-64	13 of 15
MS-65	12 of 15

The 1927 is an issue that is almost always found with a sharp strike. The obverse has very sharp detail on the feathers, but the border is sometimes a bit less well impressed with signs of buckling. The reverse is also sharp with full feathers on the breast, leg and wing, but there may be some weakness at the border.

The surfaces generally show small, scattered marks. A number of 1927 Quarter Eagles have mint-made copper spots as well. If the collector takes his time, however, he should be able to locate a coin that has only minor marks.

The luster, as on most of the Philadelphia issues from the 1920's is very good. The 1927 is generally frosty although not quite as much so as the 1926 or the 1928. Locating a specimen with good luster is reasonably easy.

The natural coloration ranges from bright rose-gold to a more subdued medium to deep green-gold. Pieces with attractive natural color are still available.

The level of eye appeal is above average. Most higher grade 1927 Quarter Eagles are well struck, have excellent color and luster and have fewer serious marks than other dates of this type.

To qualify for the Condition Census, a 1927 Indian Head Quarter Eagle must be Mint State-66.

1928

The 1928 is very similar in rarity to the 1927. It is another issue that can be located with no real difficulty in any grade up to Mint State-64. Gems are harder to find than the 1926 and the 1927 issues, but are much more available than the very underrated 1929.

Mintage: 416,000

Overall Rarity: 12 of 15

Uncirculated Rarity:

MS-62   12 of 15
MS-63   12 of 15
MS-64   12 of 15
MS-65   11 of 15

The 1928 is not usually seen with as good a strike as the 1926 and 1927 Quarter Eagles. Many pieces show centralized weakness on both the obverse and the reverse and it is not uncommon to find coins that exhibit noticeable die swelling at the borders. Some 1928 Quarter Eagles exist with sharp, even strikes and advanced collectors consider these more desirable than typical weakly struck coins.

As on most Indian Head Quarter Eagles, regardless of date, the surfaces show numerous small abrasions. It is possible to locate a 1928 with clean surfaces, but these are scarce.

The luster is excellent on most high grade pieces. It is frosty in texture and has a sort of glow that can give a choice, original piece exceptional eye appeal.

A broad range of coloration has been seen on 1928 Quarter Eagles. This ranges from rose-gold and bright yellow-gold to a deeper green-gold hue. It is still relatively easy to find a piece with good color.

The level of eye appeal for the 1928 Quarter Eagle is above average. While there are some coins that are not well struck, most have excellent luster and color. This is among the more available Indian Head Quarter Eagle in gem condition and there are some extremely pleasing pieces known to exist.

To qualify for the Condition Census, a 1928 Indian Head Quarter Eagle must be Mint State-66.

1929

The 1929 is the final Indian Head Quarter Eagle. It is also one of the more peculiar issues of this type. It is readily available in the lower Uncirculated grades and not that hard to locate in Mint State-64. But in Mint State-65 it is rare and underrated with far fewer known in this grade than any other date from the 1920's.

Mintage: 532,000

Overall Rarity: 14 of 15

Uncirculated Rarity:

MS-62   15 of 15
MS-63   15 of 15
MS-64   11 of 15
MS-65   9 of 15

Most 1929 Quarter Eagles show a good overall strike with good detail noted at the obverse and reverse centers. There are some that have minor weakness at the borders due to die buckling.

The surfaces nearly always show clusters of small marks. This is one reason why it is so difficult to find gem 1929 Quarter Eagles. A number display mint-made spots on the surfaces. These do not affect the grade or value unless they are extensive or placed in prime focal points.

The 1929 Quarter Eagle shows very good luster with a deep, frosty texture seen on original, high grade coins.

There is not as broad a range of coloration seen on this issue as the 1926-28 Quarter Eagles. Most 1929's show medium to deep yellow-gold color. A few have a more green-gold hue.

This is a very hard issue to locate in Mint State-65. The major reason for this is the abundance of marks seen on the surfaces of most 1929 Quarter Eagles. Other than this, the 1929 has good eye appeal with sharp strikes, good luster and pleasing color typically seen on higher grade pieces.

To qualify for the Condition Census, a 1929 Indian Head Quarter Eagle must be Mint State-65.

INDIAN HEAD QUARTER EAGLES - CHECK LIST

DATE - MINT	NGC	PCGS		GRADE	SMITHSONIAN* DATE - ACQUIRED	NOTES
☐ 1908	☐	☐	___	MS 63		
☐ 1909	☐	☐	___	MS 63		
☐ 1910	☐	☐	___	MS 63		
☐ 1911	☐	☐	___	MS 63		
☐ 1911-D	☐	☐	___	MS 61		
☐ 1912	☐	☐	___	MS 63		
☐ 1913	☐	☐	___	MS 64		
☐ 1914	☐	☐	___	MS 63		
☐ 1914-D	☐	☐	___	MS 64		
☐ 1915	☐	☐	___	MS 64		
☐ 1925-D	☐	☐	___	MS 63		
☐ 1926	☐	☐	___	MS 64		
☐ 1927	☐	☐	___	MS 65		
☐ 1928	☐	☐	___	MS 64		
☐ 1929	☐	☐	___	MS 64		

* Finest gold coin specimen in the National Numismatic Collection of the Smithsonian Institution

NOTES:

DATE BY DATE ANALYSIS

This date by date analysis of the Indian Head Half Eagle series goes over many topics of interest to the collector that includes a general description or history of each piece, along with comments on each issue's characteristics of strike, luster, color, and eye appeal.

Each issue includes a ranking of Overall Rarity and Uncirculated Rarity. Overall Rarity is determined by my estimate of the total number of coins that exist in all grades. Uncirculated Rarity is determined by the total number of coins that exist in MS62 - MS65 grades tabulated by total population figures supplied by PCGS and NGC.

You will find that there is no price listed under each coin as pricing information becomes dated relatively quickly. You should speak to your dealer or representative for current pricing on the coin(s) you are interested in.

Counterfeit gold coins imported from China are a growing concern to the numismatic community. Replicas are sometimes seen listed without proper identification on various online auction sites and at flea markets. Only buy Indian Gold coins from a reputable dealer and preferably authenticated and graded by either PCGS or NGC.

Specifications

$5 INDIAN HEAD HALF EAGLES

Designer: Bela Lyon Pratt

Minted From: 1908-1916 & 1929

Minted At: Philadelphia, New Orleans,
Denver and San Francisco

Diameter: 21.6 mm

Weight: 8.359 grams

Composition: .900 gold, .100 copper

Net Weight: .24187 oz pure gold

Edge: Reeded to prevent gold shaving

SYMBOLOGY

1 Inscribed around the top rim of the obverse is the word LIBERTY.

2 The obverse features the first realistic depiction of a Native American Chief in war bonnet ever used on a U.S. gold coin. Like the other devices on the coin, the Indian figure is incuse, meaning sunken rather than raised.

3 The obverse features THIRTEEN STARS representing the original colonies, which are divided by the LIBERTY device at the top rim.

4 Designer, Bela Lyon Pratt's initials, BLP.

5 The mint year date runs along the obverse's center bottom rim.

6 "UNITED STATES OF AMERICA" is inscribed around the top rim of the coin's reverse denoting the coin as US legal tender.

7 The motto "IN GOD WE TRUST" is inscribed near the right rim of the reverse just to the right of the eagle's back.

8 The central device on the reverse is a majestic eagle, which has traditionally been symbolic for the freedom represented by America.

9 The motto "E PLURIBUS UNUM", Latin for "out of many, one," is inscribed on the reverse just to the left of the eagle's breast.

10 The mint mark location is just to the left of the arrow tips. On the pictured coin, there is no mint mark, which indicates this coin was minted at Philadelphia.

11 The eagle sits atop a bundle of arrows around which is wrapped an olive branch. Together, these two symbolize America's military strength and readiness to defend its interests and its desire for peace.

12 The legal tender denomination of "FIVE DOLLARS" is inscribed along the bottom rim of the coin's reverse.

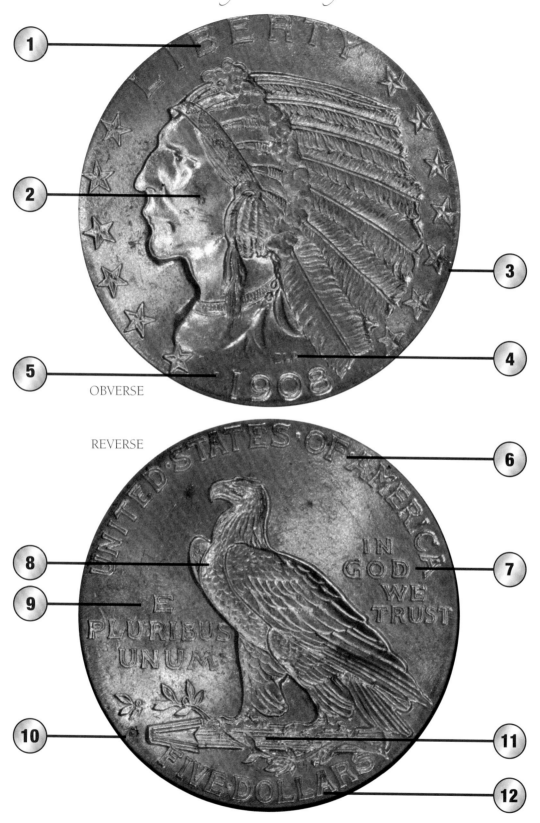

OBVERSE

REVERSE

Business Strike

Proof

1908

The 1908 is the popular first Half Eagle of this design type produced at the Philadelphia Mint. It actually has a lower mintage figure than the 1909-1913 dates but it is more available than these issues in higher grades because a fairly significant quantity was saved as first-year-of-issue souvenirs.

Mintage: 577,845 + 167 Proofs

Overall Rarity: 20 of 24

Uncirculated Rarity:

MS-62	20 of 24
MS-63	20 of 24
MS-64	23 of 24
MS-65	24 of 24

Contemporary reaction to the new Indian Head Half Eagle design was very negative but today's collectors find these coins to be among the more attractive United States gold issues ever produced.

The 1908 tends to show a good quality strike. Many have some minor weakness of strike at the centers and on the tips of a few of the feathers but this is among the better produced issues of this design.

Most 1908 Half Eagles show a number of abrasions on the surfaces. Because of the incuse design, the surfaces were very exposed and, as a result, very few exist today that are considered to be Gem coins. In addition, in the days before third-party grading many Indian Head Half Eagles were kept in albums with acetate slides that scratched the Indian's cheek whenever they were moved back and forth.

The luster ranges from very frosty to grainy in texture and frosty coins are considered the most desirable by collectors. The quality of the luster seen on the 1908 Half Eagle tends to be above-average for this design.

The natural coloration on 1908 Half Eagles is often a rich orange-gold hue but original pieces are also seen with a somewhat greenish color. It is easier to locate examples of this date with nice color than nearly any other Indian Head Half Eagle and this makes the 1908 a very popular coin with type collectors seeking a single high grade piece for their holdings.

The typical 1908 Half Eagle grades AU55 to MS62 and is characterized by heavily abraded surfaces but nice color and luster. This date becomes moderately scarce in MS63 to MS64 and MS65 examples, while genuinely scarce, are far more available than any other issue in this series. A few are known in MS66 and above and these are very rare.

There were 167 Proofs produced and it is likely that around five to six dozen of these exist. They are the least rare Indian Head Half Eagle in the PR64 to PR65 grade range and it appears that a number were saved as first-year-of-issue novelties. They are very rare in PR66 and extremely rare in any grade above this. They are characterized by a grainy texture with a dark to very dark green-gold coloration. This texture and color is similar to that seen on Indian Head Half Eagle Proofs dated 1911.

1908-D

Because of the fact that it is the first Indian Head Half Eagle struck at the Denver Mint, the 1908-D is a very popular issue. It is far scarcer than the 1908 in terms of overall rarity but comparable in the lower Uncirculated grades. It becomes much scarcer in MS64 and MS65 examples are extremely rare. In fact, the 1908-D is far rarer than the lower-mintage, more-heralded 1908-S in MS65 and above.

Mintage: 148,000

Overall Rarity: 15 of 24

Uncirculated Rarity:

MS-62	16 of 24
MS-63	23 of 24
MS-64	17 of 24
MS-65	11 of 24

The 1908-D is usually somewhat softly struck with the obverse not as well detailed as seen on the Philadelphia issue from this year. The reverse is a bit better struck but many pieces have some weakness on the feathers. The mintmark is sometimes blurry and not fully formed.

The surfaces on the 1908-D are almost always noticeably abraded. Many pieces have scratches or abrasions and finding an example that is free of detracting marks can be very difficult.

Luster on this issue is above-average with the majority of higher grade pieces showing a soft, satiny texture. This luster is rarely vibrant and many 1908-D Half Eagles have a somewhat dull appearance that might not be appealing to the collector. Flashy examples are known and these generally bring big premiums.

The natural coloration is often a medium orange-gold and rose shade. Less often, it is more green-gold in hue. It is hard to find 1908-D Half Eagles with very good color as many have been cleaned or improperly handled.

The eye appeal on this issue tends to be a bit below average. The typical example is very scuffy and has an incomplete strike. Nearly every known Uncirculated example is in the MS60 to MS62 range because of the aforementioned abrasions and clean, high end Uncirculated examples are extremely hard to locate.

This date will prove to be very challenging to the advanced collector and we really like the long-term desirability of pieces that grade MS63 and above. If you are putting together a high grade set of Indian Head Half Eagles and you have a chance to buy a coin graded MS65 you should jump at the opportunity as only one or two examples per year are typically available.

1908-S

The popular 1908-S has the lowest mintage figure of any San Francisco Half Eagle of this design. It also has the third lowest mintage of any coin of this type, trailing only the 1909-O and the 1911-D.

Mintage: 82,000

Overall Rarity: 3 of 24

Uncirculated Rarity:

MS-62	2 of 24
MS-63	9 of 24
MS-64	12 of 24
MS-65	17 of 24

Despite this issue's low mintage and its relative rarity in all grades, it is actually among the most common Indian Head Half Eagles in higher grades. There are a surprising number of Gem and Superb Gem pieces known.

The 1908-S is among the best struck San Francisco Half Eagles. Most examples show complete definition on both the obverse and reverse with strong feathers in the Indian's bonnet and bold wing and eagle detail on the eagle. The mintmark is well-defined and can be clearly seen even on lower grade examples.

The surfaces typically show some scattered marks but the 1908-S tends to come less abraded than the other San Francisco Half Eagles of this type.

The luster is excellent and it certainly ranks as one of the best San Francisco issues of this type. The texture is often soft and very frosty with an almost "velvet-like" appearance. Other pieces exist that show a satiny appearance. These two different looks are very distinctive and the same scenario exists for the 1908-S eagle.

Coloration seen on the 1908-S Half Eagle ranges from orange-gold to reddish-gold. Some examples have deeper reddish-gold color at the borders and a number of light to medium mint-made copper spots on the surfaces.

The eye appeal of this issue tends to be far above average for a San Francisco Indian Head Half Eagle. There are a number of Gems known that are very well struck, have superb color and luster and show just a few small marks on the surfaces.

The 1908-S is really the only San Francisco Half Eagle of this type that is ever available in Gem Uncirculated and it is also ranks as one of the prettiest issues in this series. It makes an excellent type coin for the collector looking for a very high grade Indian Head Half Eagle who wants something a bit more "exotic" than a common date issue from Philadelphia.

Business Strike

Proof

1909

1909 is the only year in which Indian Head Half Eagles were produced at four different mints: Philadelphia, Denver, New Orleans and San Francisco. The 1909 is the second most available of these four issues. It is very common in circulated grades and not especially scarce in the lower Uncirculated range. As with all dates of this design, examples graded MS64 and higher are very scarce and properly graded Gems are very rare. In MS65 the 1909 is comparable to the 1909-D.

Mintage: 627,060 + 78 Proofs

Overall Rarity: 18 of 24

Uncirculated Rarity:

MS-62	19 of 24
MS-63	17 of 24
MS-64	18 of 24
MS-65	22 of 24

This is generally a well struck issue with most examples showing good overall detail on both the obverse and the reverse. On a few examples, the eagle's feathers at the center of the left wing are not fully formed.

The surfaces are usually heavily abraded and many 1909 Half Eagles have detracting scratches or deep marks which are positioned in very noticeable areas. This is a very hard issue to find with choice surfaces but if the collector is patient he should be able to locate a piece that is only modestly abraded.

The luster ranges from grainy in texture to frosty. Coins that are frosty are considered more desirable but these are also more difficult to locate.

The normal coloration on 1909 Half Eagles is a warm greenish orange-gold. Examples are also seen with a more bright yellow-gold shade. It is becoming more and more difficult to find a piece with nice color and these typically trade for a premium among knowledgeable collectors.

The 1909 Half Eagle tends to have average to slightly above average eye appeal. It is a generally well produced issue with decent color and luster but most have a number of marks in the fields. This will prove to be an easy date for most collectors to locate with the exception of perfectionists who seek a coin better than MS65. In this case, the 1909 will be a very elusive member of the Indian Half Eagle set.

Only 78 Proofs were produced and it is unlikely that more than thirty or so exist. Most of these pieces are in the PR64 to PR65 range. Examples that grade PR66 and higher are extremely rare. The finish seen on Proofs of this year is referred to as Roman Gold and it is unique to gold coins dated 1909 and 1910. It is semi-brilliant with a satiny texture.

1909-D

The 1909-D is, by a large margin, the most common Indian Head Half Eagle. This makes sense given the fact that it has a mintage figure that is more than double the next highest for this design (the 1911-S). Examples of this date are still being found in overseas sources and it is likely that thousands more are waiting to enter the market. However, nearly all the examples that are being repatriated are either circulated or in the lower Uncirculated grades and Gem 1909-D Half Eagles are actually quite scarce.

Mintage: 3,423,560

Overall Rarity: 24 of 24

Uncirculated Rarity:

MS-62	24 of 24
MS-63	24 of 24
MS-64	24 of 24
MS-65	23 of 24

The 1909-D is not as well produced as some of the Philadelphia issues of this era but it is still one of the sharper Denver Half Eagles of this type. The strike is sometimes a bit weak at the centers of the obverse and reverse but the collector should be able to locate a sharp, well defined piece with relatively little effort.

On nearly every known example of this date, the surfaces show heavy abrasions. Many have deep scratches or bagmarks and finding a 1909-D Half Eagle that is clean and free of serious marks is extremely difficult. In fact, this is the reason why this otherwise common date is considered to be quite rare in MS65 and higher grades.

The luster is usually frosty and soft in its texture but many 1909-D Half Eagles have impaired luster as a result of mishandling. This is not an easy issue to find with original, undisturbed luster.

The coloration shows a very wide range of hues including reddish-gold to green-gold to rich yellow-gold. None of these are "better" than the other and it is up to the collector to decide which color he or she prefers.

The 1909-D Half Eagle has average quality eye appeal. It is a well struck issue with decent luster and color but most are seen with heavy abrasions in the fields. It is very common in MS63 and below and MS64's can certainly be found without a problem but true Gems are definitely scarce.

1909-O

The 1909-O is one of the most popular and numismatically significant issues in the entire Indian Head Half Eagle series. It is the only issue of this design produced in New Orleans and it has the lowest mintage figure of any business strike in the series.

Mintage: 34,200

Overall Rarity: 6 of 24

Uncirculated Rarity:

MS-62	1 of 24
MS-63	1 of 24
MS-64	4 of 24
MS-65	6 of 24

The overall rarity of this date has been mildly overstated in the past. The 1909-O is generally relatively available in the EF and AU grades, although nice AU55 to AU58 pieces are somewhat scarce. It is in Uncirculated that this issue becomes very scarce. Most are seen in grades MS60 to MS61 and a 1909-O in MS62 is very rare. In any grade higher than this, the 1909-O is extremely rare and Gems are among the rarest and most coveted 20th century United States gold issues. There are only two or three true Gems known and these are off the market in tightly-held collections. For all intents and purposes, the collector of high end Indian Head Half Eagles is going to have to make do with a piece in the MS62 to MS63 range.

This is a much better struck issue than most people realize with the centers usually completely detailed. The mintmark is often weak and it may show strong doubling on its left side.

The surfaces are nearly always heavily abraded and most examples show evidence of commercial use. This was clearly an issue that saw a good deal of circulation in the local economy.

The luster seen on this issue is below average with a frosty, somewhat dull texture most often seen. Most examples are worn to the point that the luster is impaired and only a few are known that exhibit very good luster.

Almost every known example has been cleaned or dipped at one time and no longer display natural coloration. On the small number of naturally toned pieces, the hues range from green-gold to orange-gold.

The 1909-O is an issue that does not have very good eye appeal. While most are well struck, this date is generally seen with a good deal of wear and very few examples are original with good color and luster. Any piece with solid overall eye appeal is worth a very strong premium.

1909-S

Although it is not as well-known as the 1909-O, the 1909-S is actually a much scarcer coin in terms of its overall rarity. The 1909-S is extremely hard to find in Uncirculated, especially in grades higher than MS62. It is rare in MS63, very rare in MS64 and extremely rare in MS65 or better.

Mintage: 297,200

Overall Rarity: 2 of 24

Uncirculated Rarity:

MS-62   6 of 24
MS-63   2 of 24
MS-64   5 of 24
MS-65   3 of 24

This is among the best struck Indian Head Half Eagles from this mint and both the obverse and reverse are typically seen with full definition. The mintmark is sharply struck and clear, unlike a number of the San Francisco issues. There are two varieties known: a perfect mintmark and a double punched mintmark. The latter is scarcer.

The surfaces are often quite abraded and show scuffmarks from careless handling. A number have light scratches or hairlines from having been cleaned at one time.

The luster is excellent with higher grade pieces displaying rich mint frost. When this date is found nice—which is really not all that often—it tends to be very attractive.

Coloration on the 1909-S Half Eagle is most often a medium to deep rose and coppery orange-gold. Many have been dipped at one time and, as a result, no longer display this pleasing rich natural coloration.

The eye appeal seen on the typical 1909-S is somewhat below average. This is mainly due to the fact that most have somewhat impaired luster. As stated above, there are some very pleasing examples known and the few Gems that exist can be considered among the more attractive San Francisco Half Eagles of this type.

1910

Business Strike

Proof

The 1910 is comparable
to the 1909 in terms of its
overall rarity but it is scarcer
in Uncirculated, especially
in grades above MS63.

Mintage: 604,000 + 250 Proofs

Overall Rarity: 17 of 24

Uncirculated Rarity:

MS-62	17 of 24
MS-63	16 of 24
MS-64	14 of 24
MS-65	15 of 24

This is a very well struck issue that generally shows complete definition on the obverse and reverse details. On a small number of pieces, there is weakness seen on the eagle's lower neck feathers and at the junction of the leg and chest.

The surfaces on most pieces show a number of scuffmarks and some have deep scratches. This is a very hard coin to find with clean surfaces but the patient collector should be able to locate a piece that does not have major detracting abrasions.

The luster seen on the 1910 Half Eagle has a soft frosty texture that tends to be a little less vibrant than that seen on the 1909 Half Eagles. A small number of 1910's are known which have a satiny texture that somewhat resembles the appearance of a Roman Finish proof.

Coloration ranges from light yellow gold and a deeper orange and green hue. Many pieces have been cleaned or dipped at one time and locating examples with original color is difficult.

This is a well made date that can be found with a good strike and excellent luster. Finding a clean piece is a much more difficult proposition but it is certainly not impossible.

The 1910 is common in the lower Uncirculated grades and only marginally scarce in MS63. It becomes very scarce in MS64 and it is very rare in MS65. In grades above this, the 1910 is almost unknown.

A total of 250 Proofs were produced, using the distinctive Roman Finish that is also seen on 1909 Proofs. It is likely that many examples were unsold and later melted and this issue is comparable in rarity to the 1909. Most grade PR64 to PR65 and pieces in PR66 and above are extremely rare.

1910-D

The 1910-D is a relatively common issue in the Indian Head Half Eagle series but it is scarcer than generally realized in higher grades. Most pieces grade AU55 to MS62. It is moderately scarce in MS63 but it becomes very scarce in MS64 and it is very rare in properly graded MS65. Most of the lower grade Uncirculated 1910-D Half Eagles are from a few small hoards that were found in the late 1970's/early 1980's.

Mintage: 193,600

Overall Rarity: 9 of 24

Uncirculated Rarity:

MS-62   11 of 24
MS-63   13 of 24
MS-64   9 of 24
MS-65   7 of 24

While not as well struck as the 1909-D, this is still a well produced issue that shows good definition on the headdress and eagle's feathers. The mintmark is found in two distinct variations. The more common examples have a high relief mintmark that is not well-defined and which has a closed appearance. The scarcer variety has a lower relief mintmark which is more open and better defined.

The surfaces are less abraded on examples of this date than on other Denver Half Eagles of this era. That said it is still very difficult to find a 1910-D that does not show a number of scuffs and/or abrasions in the fields.

The luster is very good with most pieces exhibiting a satiny texture. A smaller number have a soft, frosty texture. Both of these are considered desirable by collectors.

There is a very wide variety of colors seen on this issue. This ranges from rich rose-gold to orange to green-gold. It should be possible to find a 1910-D with good color.

The 1910-D has slightly better than average eye appeal. It is a generally well struck issue although some pieces are weak on the mintmark. Collectors should be able to locate a nice, appealing MS63 to MS64 but locating a properly graded Gem is extremely difficult. This date is comparable in high grade rarity to the 1914-D but it is not as rare as the undervalued 1908-D.

1910-S

The 1910-S is by far the scarcest of the three Half Eagles produced in this year. It is very similar in overall and high grade rarity to the 1912-S.

Mintage: : 770,200

Overall Rarity: 5 of 24

Uncirculated Rarity:

MS-62	7 of 24
MS-63	5 of 24
MS-64	7 of 24
MS-65	8 of 24

It has been mentioned in print that this is not a well struck issue but this is not the case. The 1910-S Half Eagle generally shows very good detail on both the obverse and the reverse. The mintmark is better defined than on the later date San Francisco Half Eagles of this design on which the mintmark is often very blurry.

The surfaces are generally noticeably abraded with a number of pieces showing detracting marks and abrasions in the fields. Some have mint-made spotting on the surfaces and it is very hard to find a piece that is clean.

Luster on this issue is found with two distinct textures. The more common of these is soft and very frosty while the second is very satiny. Both are desirable; although the latter is found on most of the very high grade certified 1910-S Half Eagles.

A range of coloration can be found on original, uncleaned pieces. Hues seen on this date include rose, orange and an unusual and very attractive pale copper shade. Higher grade 1910-S Half Eagles can be among the best looking coins of this design from the San Francisco Mint.

The level of eye appeal for this date is better than one might expect. The strike is usually good as are the color and luster. Most pieces are noticeably marked and this is why the typical Uncirculated 1910-S is in the MS60 to MS62 range. The 1910-S is extremely scarce in MS63, rare in MS64 and very rare in MS65.

1911

Business Strike

Proof

The 1911 is among the more common Indian Head Half Eagles. It is seen more often than the 1909 and the 1910 and it is comparable to the 1908 except in higher grades, in which it is decidedly rarer.

Mintage: 915,000 + 139 Proofs

Overall Rarity: 21 of 24

Uncirculated Rarity:

MS-62	21 of 24
MS-63	19 of 24
MS-64	20 of 24
MS-65	20 of 24

This is among the worst struck dates of this design. The feathers often show weakness and the bonnet may have some blurry areas where the details are not fully brought up. The reverse is better struck but many pieces show weakness on the eagle's left (facing) wing. It is possible to find pieces that show a better strike than average and the collector who finds it important to own a sharp coin is urged to be patient and wait for the right piece.

The surfaces are usually abraded but it is possible to find a 1911 Half Eagle that has only minor marks. The 1911 has granular surfaces which are different in appearance from most other Philadelphia gold coins of this design.

The luster is below average. It is subdued in appearance with a slightly grainy appearance and it lacks the "pizzazz" seen on other Philadelphia Half Eagles.

A wide range of coloration has been observed on this date. Most 1911 Half Eagles are light to medium greenish-gold but others have light orange-gold hues which can be very attractive.

The eye appeal on this issue tends to be below average. Many 1911 Half Eagles are not well struck and have granular surfaces with somewhat dull luster. There are some pretty pieces known, however, and these generally bring a premium when they are offered for sale.

A total of 139 Proofs were struck. These coins have a dark matte finish like the 1908 but with a slightly different texture. In terms of rarity, Proofs of this year are similar to the 1910. There are probably three to four dozen known with most of these in the PR63 to PR65 range. A few are known in PR66 and PR67 grades and these are very rare.

1911-D

While the similarly dated quarter eagle is a much better known issue, the 1911-D Half Eagle is a far rarer coin in high grades. It is the fourth rarest Indian Head Half Eagle in Gem Uncirculated, trailing only the 1912-S, 1913-S and 1914-S, and it must be considered among the prime rarities among all 20th century United States gold coinage in MS65 and higher grades.

Mintage: 72,500

Overall Rarity: 7 of 24

Uncirculated Rarity:

MS-62	3 of 24
MS-63	7 of 24
MS-64	6 of 24
MS-65	9 of 24

As with nearly all gold coins produced at the Denver Mint, this is a well struck issue that shows good detail on both the obverse and the reverse. The mintmark is in very low relief but it is clear to the naked eye.

The surfaces are always seen with a grainy appearance and this tends to give the 1911-D Half Eagle a very distinctive appearance. In addition to this granularity, the surfaces normally are very heavily abraded. This issue appears to have seen greater circulation than other Denver Mint Half Eagles of the early 1910's and many examples are visibly worn from commercial use.

The luster is among the worst found on any Indian Head Half Eagle. As a result of the way the dies were prepared; it is typically very grainy in appearance and lacks the vibrancy seen on the earlier Denver Half Eagles.

The coloration is most often a light green-gold. A few 1911-D Half Eagles have orange-gold hues. Many examples have been cleaned or dipped and locating pieces with original color is very challenging.

The level of eye appeal for this issue is well below average. The typical 1911-D has inferior luster and grainy surfaces with a sort of "washed-out" appearance.

The 1911-D is not a scarce coin in circulated grades and it can be found in the lower Uncirculated grades without much of an effort. It becomes very scarce in MS62 and it is very rare in MS63. In MS64, this issue is extremely rare and the population figures listed by both PCGS and NGC are extremely inflated due to resubmissions.

1911-S

The 1911-S has the second highest mintage figure of any date in this series. But it is not a common issue. In fact, the 1911-S is scarce enough to suggest that a number of these were melted.

Mintage: 1,416,000

Overall Rarity: 13 of 24

Uncirculated Rarity:

MS-62	14 of 24
MS-63	11 of 24
MS-64	8 of 24
MS-65	10 of 24

The strike seen on the obverse is sometimes a bit weak on the tips of the feathers, especially the bottom four. The rest of the obverse details are sharp, including the headdress. The reverse is more boldly impressed with good feather and wing detail. The mintmark is small and often well defined. A few are known with mintmarks that are "blobby" in appearance and not sharply defined.

The surfaces usually show numerous abrasions. This is an issue that is extremely hard to find with clean, original surfaces and many pieces show hairlines from old cleanings or evidence of having been mishandled.

The luster on this issue is not very good when compared to the other San Francisco Half Eagles of this type. It is typically a bit on the drab side and usually frosty in texture.

Coloration on the 1911-S Half Eagle is invariably orange-gold with a slightly reddish tint. There are a decent number of pieces available with original color and the collector should be able to locate one with some patience.

The 1911-S is an issue with slightly below average to average quality eye appeal. Some examples are not well struck on the obverse and most have somewhat subdued luster. The typical piece grades in the AU55 to MS62 range which was reflected by a small deal of these that were recently well distributed. MS-65 specimens are rare and prized when located.

Business Strike

Proof

1912

The 1912 is one of the more common Philadelphia Half Eagles in terms of overall rarity. In high grades, it is much rarer than the 1908 and 1909 and comparable to the 1911 and the 1913 but much more available than the underrated 1910.

Mintage: : 790,000 + 144 Proofs

Overall Rarity: 22 of 24

Uncirculated Rarity:

MS-62	22 of 24
MS-63	21 of 24
MS-64	19 of 24
MS-65	19 of 24

This is an extremely well produced issue that is almost always found with full detail on the obverse and the reverse. It is an excellent choice for type purposes because of this fact.

The surfaces usually are heavily abraded. This is really the case with essentially all of the issues in this series. This is due to the design of the Indian Head Half Eagle and the fact that these coins tended to be treated very roughly when they were being shipped from the U.S. Mint to local banks.

The luster on this issue is above average but it tends to be grainy in texture and not frosty like on the earlier Philadelphia Half Eagles of this design. Some pieces have a subdued appearance and the collector who likes bright, flashy coins may have to wait a while before the right 1912 Half Eagle becomes available.

1912 Half Eagles are usually seen with a very distinctive green-gold hue. This color is different than that found on most other Philadelphia Indian Head Half Eagles and it gives this date a unique, distinctive appearance.

The 1912 Half Eagle has average eye appeal. It is well struck and tends to have good luster but, as mentioned above, its appearance is very distinctive and this look may not appeal to all collectors.

This is a common date in all Uncirculated grades up to and including MS63. MS64 pieces are scarce and MS-65's are rare. Unlike the 1908 and the 1909, this is a date that is nearly unknown above MS65 and the connoisseur will be lucky to find an accurately graded MS65.

There were 144 Proofs struck. They use a fine sandblast finish which is similar to that seen on the 1913. An estimated 35-45 Proofs are known with most of these in the PR64 to PR66 range. There are more very high grade Proofs known of this date than any other Indian Head Half Eagle with a number known that grade PR67. These remarkable coins are popular with type collectors seeking a single very high grade Proof Indian Head Half Eagle for their set.

1912-S

In 1912 and 1913, the number of mints striking Indian Head Half Eagles was reduced from three to two as the Denver Mint did not produce any of these coins. The 1912-S is among the scarcer San Francisco Half Eagles of this design.

Mintage: 392,000

Overall Rarity: 8 of 24

Uncirculated Rarity:

MS-62   5 of 24
MS-63   3 of 24
MS-64   10 of 24
MS-65   4 of 24

Of all the issues of this design, the 1912-S is most likely to show strike problems. The obverse typically is weak at the border as a result of die deterioration. There is often what appears to be an area of die sinking sticking out from the date and this extends far to the left, up to the stars. The reverse also shows weakness at the border and this tends to affect the mintmark which tends to be very weakly detailed. On a number of 1912-S Half Eagles, the mintmark appears to be little more than a blob which can be hard to distinguish as being an "S." There are some examples that show a better than average strike but for the most part this is an issue that will prove to be very frustrating for the collector who requires a boldly detailed coin.

Most 1912-S Half Eagles are very heavily abraded and show detracting marks in the fields. This is a very hard issue to find with clean surfaces.

The luster found on this issue tends to be satiny in texture and very subdued. It is far less appealing than that seen on the earlier San Francisco Half Eagles of this type.

The coloration tends to be light to medium reddish gold with an orange overtone. On original, higher grade pieces this coloration is quite attractive.

The level of eye appeal seen on this date is among the worst for any in the series. Most 1912-S Half Eagles are poorly struck, have dull luster and show numerous marks on the surfaces. Any piece with good eye appeal is extremely scarce and is worth a strong premium.

This date is scarce in any Uncirculated grade and it becomes very scarce in MS62. The 1912-S is rare in MS63, very rare in MS64 and extremely rare in MS65.

1913

Business Strike

Proof

The 1913 is the second most common Indian Head Half Eagle in terms of overall rarity. In MS63 and above it is quite a bit scarcer than issues such as the 1908 and 1909-D and it is very comparable in this grade range to the 1912.

Mintage: 915,901 + 99 Proofs

Overall Rarity: 23 of 24

Uncirculated Rarity:

MS-62	23 of 24
MS-63	22 of 24
MS-64	21 of 24
MS-65	21 of 24

This issue tends to be quite well struck with very good overall detail seen on the obverse and on the reverse. On some pieces there is slight weakness on the eagle's left (facing) leg but the collector should be able to find a well struck example with very little problem.

The surfaces are often noticeably abraded with deep, detracting marks. But there are a decent number of reasonably clean pieces and some very choice, relatively mark-free examples trade from time to time.

The luster is finely granular in texture, as seen on the 1912 Half Eagle.

Coloration on the 1913 Half Eagle is often a distinctive greenish-gold in hue and, less often a nice medium orange-gold shade. There are a decent number of attractive, original coins that still display pleasing coloration available to the collector.

The 1913 Half Eagle shows good eye appeal. The average example is well struck, has decent luster and color and suffers only from some marks on the surfaces.

This date has become more available in recent years due to a number of decent sized hoards coming onto the market. It is common in grades up to and including MS63. It is scarce in MS64 and rare in MS65.

There were 99 Proofs struck in 1913, of which an estimated thirty to forty are still known. These are found with the same color and finish as on the 1912 Proofs. Most are seen in the PR64 to PR65 range with a few known in grades as high as PR66 to PR67.

1913-S

At one time the 1913-S was considered to be one of the rarest dates in the series in terms of its overall rarity. There have been a number of pieces that have been found in overseas sources in the past few years but these are generally circulated coins or low end Uncirculated examples that grade no better than MS60 to MS61. This date remains a major rarity in the higher grades.

Mintage: 408,000

Overall Rarity: 11 of 24

Uncirculated Rarity:

MS-62	9 of 24
MS-63	8 of 24
MS-64	3 of 24
MS-65	5 of 24

This date is not as poorly struck as the 1912-S but it still shows one of the worst strikes of any date in this series. As on the 1912-S, there is noticeable die deterioration at the borders that gives them a sunken appearance. The mintmark on many 1913-S Half Eagles is quite weak and appears to be more of a blob than the letter "S." A number of examples are also not fully defined at the centers and there may be weakness on the bonnet and on the eagle's feathers, especially near the legs.

Most 1913-S Half Eagles have heavily abraded surfaces with most pieces showing detracting marks, often in such prime focal places as on the Indian's cheek and in the left obverse field.

The luster on this issue is probably the poorest on any Indian Head Half Eagle. It is usually dull and even higher grade coins tend to not have the vibrancy seen on the earlier San Francisco issues of this type.

1913-S Half Eagles are often found with a light orange-gold and rose coloration. A number of lower grade pieces have a "dirty" appearance, probably as a result of improper storage in bags or bank vaults.

The level of eye appeal on this date is below average and, along with the 1912-S, it is probably the hardest Indian Head Half Eagle to find with a good overall appearance. There are a very small number of pieces known that are well struck and have good color and these typically command enormous premiums on the infrequent occasions they are offered for sale.

The 1913-S Half Eagle is usually seen in AU grades and it is scarce in the lower Uncirculated grades. It becomes extremely scarce in MS63 and it is very rare in MS65. Gems are extremely rare.

1914

Business Strike

Proof

The 1914 is the second scarcest Philadelphia Half Eagle of this type, trailing only the 1929. It has never really commanded much of a premium over such very common dates as the 1908, 1909 and 1909-D and many experts consider it to be an undervalued sleeper issue in higher grades.

Mintage: 247,000 + 125 Proofs

Overall Rarity: 16 of 24

Uncirculated Rarity:

MS-62	15 of 24
MS-63	15 of 24
MS-64	15 of 24
MS-65	16 of 24

The strike seen on this issue is very sharp with both the obverse and the reverse typically displaying complete definition including sharp feather detail in the bonnet and on the eagle's wings and legs.

The surfaces are often significantly abraded but, for some reason, many 1914 Half Eagles are seen with less detracting marks than on the earlier Philadelphia issues of this design. There are a few pieces known that are very clean and can be called Gems by anyone's standards.

The luster is not as good as that seen on the earlier Philadelphia issues but it still tends to be slightly better than average. It is generally frosty in texture and it lacks the semi-granular appearance seen on the 1912 and 1913 Half Eagles.

The coloration on the 1914 rivals any date in the series. A number of hues have been observed, ranging from bright orange-gold to medium green to rich coppery-rose. The collector who appreciates nice coloration should be able to locate a 1914 Half Eagle which offers great appeal.

The level of eye appeal for this date ranges from average to above-average. Most pieces are well struck and have decent surfaces and nice color but it is hard to find examples with good coloration.

The 1914 is common in MS60 to MS62 and only marginally scarce in MS63. Properly graded MS64 pieces are scarcer than generally realized and MS-65 coins are quite rare and very undervalued.

The original mintage figure for Proofs of this date is 125. Given the rarity of these, it is possible that a number were melted in 1914 due to not having been sold. There are probably no more than 30 or so known with most grading PR64 to PR65. A small number of PR66 pieces are known and these are extremely rare. The 1914 Proofs have a coarse sandblast finish which is similar to that seen on the 1915 and unique to these two years.

1914-D

Production of Indian Head Half Eagles at the Denver Mint was resumed in 1914 after a two year hiatus. It is interesting to note that the 1914-D has the exact same mintage figure as the 1914 (probably a coincidence) and these two issues are fairly similar in terms of their overall rarity. The 1914-D is also a numismatically significant issue as it is the final Indian Head Half Eagle produced at the Denver Mint.

Mintage: 247,000

Overall Rarity: 14 of 24

Uncirculated Rarity:

	MS-62	13 of 24
	MS-63	14 of 24
	MS-64	16 of 24
	MS-65	14 of 24

This is among the better produced Denver Indian Head Half Eagles and it shows a very bold strike on the obverse and the reverse. On a few coins, the mintmark can be somewhat poorly defined but it should be easy for the collector to find a piece with good detail on the obverse and the reverse.

The surfaces are usually peppered with a number of small abrasions. There is also some light mint-made granularity on the surfaces as on a few of the earlier Denver Half Eagles of this design.

The luster is somewhat below average. It tends to show a subdued semi-granular texture that is not usually appealing to collectors. There are some pieces known that are less granular than others and these tend to be very popular due to their better eye appeal.

The coloration found on this issue tends to be a medium to deep greenish-gold with orange-gold undertones. A few show very attractive coppery-rose color and these are considered to be the most desirable 1914-D Half Eagles.

The level of eye appeal for the 1914-D is slightly below average. Most seen have good overall detail and decent color but tend to be a bit granular in texture and have below average luster. When a very attractive piece is offered to collectors, it generally brings well in excess of current published catalog values.

In the lower Uncirculated grades, the 1914-D Half Eagle is common and even MS63 pieces are fairly easy to locate. In MS64 this date is moderately scarce and compares favorably to the 1914. In MS65 it is quite rare and is harder to locate than its Philadelphia counterpart.

1914-S

The 1914-S is one of the true "condition rarities" in the Indian Head eagle series. It is very comparable to the 1913-S in terms of overall rarity but it is far rarer in high grades and in MS64 it ranks not only as the rarest date in this series but one of the rarest 20th century gold coins of any denomination.

Mintage: 263,000

Overall Rarity: 10 of 24

Uncirculated Rarity:

MS-62	10 of 24
MS-63	4 of 24
MS-64	1 of 24
MS-65	1 of 24

The quality of strike seen on the 1914-S is better than on the 1912-S and the 1913-S but not as sharp as on the earlier San Francisco issues of this type. The centers are basically well defined although some pieces have slight weakness on the inner band of the headdress and on the eagle's left (facing) leg. The mintmark is typically very weak and it appears as a blob. On some examples, it is so weak that it can be easily overlooked. There are a small number known with sharp mintmarks and these are worth a strong premium over typical strikes.

On nearly all known examples, the surfaces are very heavily marked and there are often deep, detracting abrasions on the cheek of the Indian and in the left obverse field.

The luster on most 1914-S Half Eagles is below average. It is typically dull with a granular look. There are a few pieces known that have very good frosty luster and these pieces invariably bring a significant premium because of their excellent appearance.

The coloration most often seen on 1914-S Half Eagles is a rich orange-gold hue. This is quite attractive and very distinctive in appearance. But most have been cleaned or dipped at one time and examples with very good color are extremely scarce and desirable.

The 1914-S Half Eagle has below average eye appeal. The strike is not good, although there is less die deterioration at the borders than on the 1912-S and the 1913-S. Most pieces are heavily abraded and are dull. Any 1914-S Half Eagle with good eye appeal is quite rare and this is unquestionably the hardest issue in this series to find in grades above MS63.

Most 1914-S Half Eagles are found in AU50 to AU58 grades. This date is scarce in the lower Uncirculated range and scarce in MS62. It is quite rare in properly graded MS63 and very rare in MS64. Given the fact that these populations include some resubmissions and crossovers, the actual number of coins graded may be much less.

1915

Business Strike

Proof

The 1915 is the second to last Indian Head Half Eagle struck at the Philadelphia Mint. It is among the more common issues in the series in terms of its overall rarity but it is far scarcer in high grades than issues such as the 1908, 1909, 1911 and 1913.

Mintage: 588,000 + 75 Proofs

Overall Rarity: 19 of 24

Uncirculated Rarity:

MS-62	18 of 24
MS-63	18 of 24
MS-64	22 of 24
MS-65	18 of 24

This is an extremely well made issue which generally shows a very sharp strike on both the obverse and the reverse. Both the centers and the peripheries are nicely defined with strong details.

The surfaces are often very slightly granular but not as much so as on the 1914 Half Eagles. Many pieces have a number of abrasions but it is possible to find an example that is relatively clean.

The luster is extremely good and, in fact, it rivals nearly any issue in the series. It is sometimes extremely frosty and other times it is grainy with a good deal of "flash."

A wide range of colors have been seen on original, uncleaned pieces. The hues most often observed are green and rose-orange. A small amount of unusual—and really attractive—coppery hued pieces are known as well.

The 1915 Half Eagle has very good overall eye appeal. It is well struck and has good luster and often shows pretty coloration. Most pieces are abraded but the collector should be able to locate a piece that is relatively clean and high end without a great deal of searching.

The 1915 is common in lower Uncirculated grades and fairly easy to find even in MS63 and MS64. It is quite scarce in MS65. Interestingly, older references on Indian Head gold coinage state a small number of "superb, nearly perfect" pieces are known but these have either not been seen by the grading services or are now regarded as MS65.

Only 75 Proofs were struck, giving this the lowest mintage figure of any proof issue of this series. These are very rare with probably no more than 15-20 pieces known. Nearly all of these are in the PR64 to PR65 range. They show a coarse sandblast finish as seen on the 1914 Proofs.

1915-S

The quality problems which the San Francisco Mint suffered through when producing Half Eagles in 1913 and 1914 were somehow cured in 1915 and the 1915-S Half Eagle is a well struck issue which can be found with much better eye appeal than its predecessors. This is among the rarest dates in the series and it compares favorably with the 1914-S as the key San Francisco issue of this type.

Mintage: 164,000

Overall Rarity: 4 of 24

Uncirculated Rarity:

MS-62	8 of 24
MS-63	6 of 24
MS-64	2 of 24
MS-65	2 of 24

As mentioned this is a well struck date. The obverse sometimes shows weakness on the feathers in the headdress, especially the first two or three. The reverse is generally well detailed with strong feathers. The mintmark on most 1915-S Half Eagles is weak and on some it appears as a blob with virtually no definition. Examples with strong mintmarks are worth a premium and are very scarce. There is often some die deterioration at the borders but it is not as pronounced as that seen on the 1913-S and 1914-S Half Eagles.

This is an issue that is nearly always found with noticeable abrasions on the surfaces. Any piece that is relatively clean is very scarce and is considered very desirable by specialists in the series.

The luster on this issue is seen with a number of distinct looks. The most common texture is very frosty but others exist that are satiny with a touch of granularity. One of these is not necessarily considered better than the other but most collectors prefer the frosty look.

Coloration on this issue is most often a medium to deep orange-gold. Some of the grainy examples have a more greenish-gold hue. Many 1915-S Half Eagles have been cleaned at one time and pieces with nice original color are very scarce.

The 1915-S Half Eagle has slightly below average eye appeal. The typical piece shows die deterioration at the border and has a weak mintmark as a result. Many are very heavily abraded as well. Examples with good eye appeal are very rare.

This date is usually seen in AU grades and lower end Uncirculated examples are about the best that are generally offered for sale. The 1915-S Half Eagle is extremely scarce in properly graded MS63 and it is very rare in MS64.

1916-S

The 1916-S is the final Indian Head Half Eagle produced at the San Francisco Mint. It is the only date of this denomination to be produced in 1916, so it is an essential issue for collectors who are putting together year sets. After this issue was produced, there would be no more Indian Head Half Eagles struck until 1929.

Mintage: 240,000

Overall Rarity: 12 of 24

Uncirculated Rarity:

MS-62	12 of 24
MS-63	12 of 24
MS-64	11 of 24
MS-65	13 of 24

The 1916-S was formerly very rare in higher grades but a hoard of several hundred coins was uncovered in El Salvador in the late 1970's/early 1980's. Today, it is obtainable in grades up to and including MS64.

This is the best struck of the late date Indian Head Half Eagles from San Francisco. This issue tends to not display the die deterioration at the borders that is seen on the issues produced from 1912 through 1915. The obverse is very well struck. The reverse is a little less sharp and on some pieces the mintmark is blobby and indistinct.

Many 1916-S Half Eagles have heavily abraded surfaces. Pieces that are from the hoard mentioned above tend to show some bagmarks or other scattered abrasions in the fields. Unlike some of the earlier San Francisco Half Eagles of this design, it is possible for the collector to locate a reasonably clean piece for his set if he is patient

The luster is usually below average and it has a subdued, frosty texture with some granularity seen in the fields.

Examples of this date that are from the hoard are characterized by nice orange-gold and green coloration. Others show hues that tend more towards coppery-rose shadings.

This date tends to have reasonably good eye appeal. It is generally seen with an acceptable strike and nice color but many pieces do not have great luster.

The 1916-S is fairly easy to obtain in the lower Uncirculated grades and can with some effort be found even in MS63. It is very scarce in properly graded MS64 and very rare in MS65.

1929

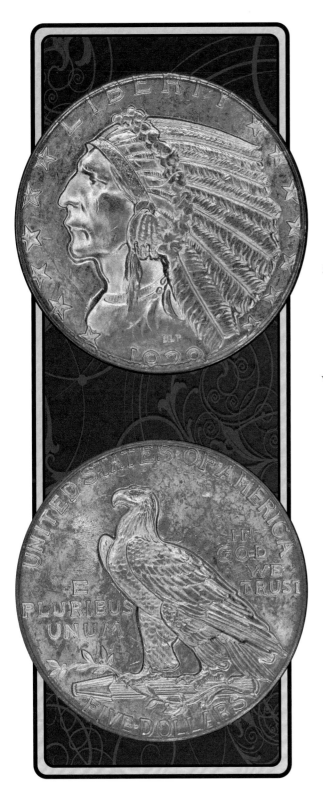

After a thirteen year hiatus, production of Indian Head Half Eagles resumed for one year only. The 1929 is one of the more popular and curious issues of this design. It is the rarest date in the series, from the standpoint of overall rarity, despite a comparatively high original mintage figure. The vast majority of 1929 Half Eagles were never released into circulation and they appear to have been melted soon afterwards. Today, this issue is almost never seen in circulated grades.

Mintage: 662,000

Overall Rarity: 1 of 24

Uncirculated Rarity:

MS-62	4 of 24
MS-63	10 of 24
MS-64	13 of 24
MS-65	12 of 24

The 1929 has a very distinctive pattern of strike. The centers are generally sharp with good details seen on the feathers and on the wings. Most examples display an indented line that runs along a good deal of the inner edge. This is most prominent through the date and in the words STATES OF on the reverse. It is possible that a 1929 Half Eagle exists without these indentations but these are a good test as to the authenticity of this issue.

Most known examples are very heavily bagmarked on the surfaces. The typical 1929 Half Eagle has the appearance of a Very Choice or even Gem piece but they are typically downgraded one or two points by the presence of detracting abrasions in the fields.

The luster on this issue is excellent and it generally has a very frosty texture. A few are seen with a more subdued satiny texture. Most collectors prefer the former surface texture.

Coloration seen on the 1929 Half Eagle is often a deep yellow-gold with strong yellowish tints. Less often, this date shows a medium green-gold hue.

The level of eye appeal on the 1929 Half Eagle is above-average. As mentioned above, examples generally have indented lines on the obverse and reverse which are mint-made. The surfaces are usually very abraded but the color and luster tend to be quite good.

The 1929 Half Eagle is an issue that did not see much—if any—circulation and it is almost never seen below the AU58 to MS60 range. It is scarce in the lower Uncirculated grades and very scarce in MS63. MS64 examples are popular and rare, despite the current PCGS/NGC population figures which appear to be highly inflated. MS-65's are very rare.

$5 Indian Head Half Eagles - Check List

DATE - MINT	NGC	PCGS	GRADE	SMITHSONIAN*	DATE - ACQUIRED	NOTES
☐ 1908	☐	☐	_____	MS 62	_____	_____
☐ 1908-D	☐	☐	_____	EF 45	_____	_____
☐ 1908-S	☐	☐	_____	EF 40	_____	_____
☐ 1909	☐	☐	_____	AU 58	_____	_____
☐ 1909-D	☐	☐	_____	MS 63	_____	_____
☐ 1909-O	☐	☐	_____	MS 65	_____	_____
☐ 1909-S	☐	☐	_____	MS 66	_____	_____
☐ 1910	☐	☐	_____	MS 60	_____	_____
☐ 1910-D	☐	☐	_____	MS 66	_____	_____
☐ 1910-S	☐	☐	_____	MS 64	_____	_____
☐ 1911	☐	☐	_____	MS 62	_____	_____

NOTES:

_____

_____

_____

* Finest gold coin specimen in the National Numismatic Collection of the Smithsonian Institution

DATE - MINT	NGC	PCGS		GRADE SMITHSONIAN*	DATE - ACQUIRED	NOTES
☐ 1911-D ☐ ☐			___	MS 65		_____
☐ 1911-S ☐ ☐			___	MS 64		_____
☐ 1912 ☐ ☐			___	MS 64		_____
☐ 1912-S ☐ ☐			___	MS 65		_____
☐ 1913 ☐ ☐			___	MS 60		_____
☐ 1913-S ☐ ☐			___	EF 40		_____
☐ 1914 ☐ ☐			___	MS 61		_____
☐ 1914-D ☐ ☐			___	MS 63		_____
☐ 1914-S ☐ ☐			___	MS 62		_____
☐ 1915 ☐ ☐			___	MS 64		_____
☐ 1915-S ☐ ☐			___	AU Cleaned		_____
☐ 1916-S ☐ ☐			___	MS 66		_____
☐ 1929 ☐ ☐			___	MS 63		_____

NOTES:

_____

_____

_____

* Finest gold coin specimen in the National Numismatic Collection of the Smithsonian Institution

DATE BY DATE ANALYSIS

This date by date analysis of the Indian Head Eagle series goes over many topics of interest to the collector that includes a general description or history of each piece, along with comments on each issue's characteristics of strike, luster, color, and eye appeal.

Each issue includes a ranking of Overall Rarity and Uncirculated Rarity. Overall Rarity is determined by my estimate of the total number of coins that exist in all grades. Uncirculated Rarity is determined by the total number of coins that exist in MS62 - MS65 grades tabulated by total population figures supplied by PCGS and NGC.

You will find that there is no price listed under each coin as pricing information becomes dated relatively quickly. You should speak to your dealer or representative for current pricing on the coin(s) you are interested in.

Counterfeit gold coins imported from China are a growing concern to the numismatic community. Replicas are sometimes seen listed without proper identification on various online auction sites and at flea markets. Only buy Indian Gold coins from a reputable dealer and preferably authenticated and graded by either PCGS or NGC.

Specifications

$10 INDIAN HEAD EAGLES

Designer: Augustus Saint-Gaudens

Minted From: 1907-1916, 1920, 1926, 1930, 1932 & 1933

Minted At: Philadelphia, Denver and San Francisco

Diameter: 27 mm

Weight: 16.718 grams

Composition: .900 gold, .100 copper

Net Weight: .48375 oz pure gold

Edge: Reeded 46 raised stars (1907 -1911) and 48 raised stars (1912-1933) representing the states in the Union.

SYMBOLOGY

1 Inscribed around the rim of the obverse are THIRTEEN STARS denoting the original 13 colonies of the United States.

2 The head of the Indian figure is crowned with an Indian War Bonnet held together by a band, which carries the inscription LIBERTY.

3 Saint-Gaudens used a classical Liberty profile rather than an authentic Indian for his main obverse device.

4 The mint year date is inscribed along the obverse rim at the bottom center.

5 "UNITED STATES OF AMERICA" is inscribed around the top rim of the coin's reverse denoting the coin as US legal tender.

6 The motto "E PLURIBUS UNUM", which is Latin for "out of many, one," is inscribed on the reverse just above the eagle's back.

7 The central device on the reverse is a majestic eagle, which has traditionally been symbolic for the freedom represented by America.

8 The motto "IN GOD WE TRUST" is inscribed near the left rim of the reverse just to the left of the eagle's breast.

9 The mint mark location is just to the left of the arrow tips (or above on the 1908-D No Motto). On the pictured coin, there is a "D" mint mark, which indicates this coin was minted at Denver.

10 The eagle sits atop a bundle of arrows around which is wrapped an olive branch. Together, these two symbolize America's military strength and readiness to defend its interests and its desire for peace.

11 The legal tender denomination of "TEN DOLLARS" is inscribed along the bottom rim of the coin's reverse.

OBVERSE

REVERSE

1907

Wire Rim

Also recognized as Judd-1774, the 1907 Wire Rim Eagles are technically considered to be special issues but they are collected alongside with the other dates in the series. They most closely represent the original concept which sculptor Augustus Saint-Gaudens and President Theodore Roosevelt imagined the new Indian Head coins to look like.

Mintage: **500**

Overall Rarity: **5 of 32**

Uncirculated Rarity:

MS-62	5 of 32
MS-63	11 of 32
MS-64	20 of 32
MS-65	22 of 32

Saint-Gaudens designed the coin with a neck-up rendition of Miss Liberty that was fashioned from inspiration attained while viewing Nike standing prominently in front of General William Tecumseh Sherman's horse at the Sherman Monument in New York City in 1905.

He felt that a full figured Liberty was more appropriate to be displayed on the larger Double Eagles for which he is most famous. At the request of President Theodore Roosevelt, Saint-Gaudens added a war bonnet to Liberty's head to give more character to the coin.

The issue gets its "Wire Rim" name from the way in which metal was squeezed between the collar and the dies, creating a knife-like rim that is prevalent on both sides of the coin. The Mint soon discovered ejection problems caused by the lack of a traditional rim. This made the issue particularly susceptible to marks and abrasions and officials ultimately decided that it was too impractical for circulation.

This transitional issue is extremely popular amongst collectors and continually commands a premium each time it is seen at auction. Gem Uncirculated (MS65) and finer examples can be found from time to time. A single MS69 example exists and it has been graded by NGC. Together with a single 1908-S, they represent the only two coins in the series to achieve that outstanding level of preservation.

Most 1907 Wire Edge Eagles are found with such outstanding strikes that their classification as Mint State coins and not as Proofs is sometimes contested. All examples known possess virtually the same appearance of strike overall.

Although many examples have numerous abrasions and dings from rough handling over the past 100 years, there are many premium pieces that are remarkably well preserved and mark-free. All Indian Head Eagles of this variety display swirl-like die polishing marks in the fields that actually add brightness to the coins.

The luster on these pieces is almost always extraordinary and is most often described as bright and heavily frosted.

The natural coloration is a rich yellow-gold but there are also a number that can be found with a beautiful reddish patina.

These coins can always be found for a price but any nice example is sure to hold a prominent role in any major collection of U.S. gold.

Probably more than half of the original mintage figure of 500 coins is still known to exist. The 1907 Wire Edge is most often seen in MS61 to MS64 grades. Gems are scarce but are more obtainable than a number of other dates in this series. A few superb pieces are known and these are among the most highly prized issues in the entire series.

1907
Rolled Edge

The 1907 Rolled Edge variety were the first Indian Eagles struck that were initially intended for circulation. Mint Engraver Charles Barber recognized a need to create a more traditional rim so the coins would stack properly after being ejected and his concept gained swift approval.

Mintage: "50"
(31,500 struck but most were melted down)

Overall Rarity: 2 of 32

Uncirculated Rarity:

MS-62	2 of 32
MS-63	2 of 32
MS-64	2 of 32
MS-65	15 of 32

Approximately 31,500 were originally struck but nearly all were destroyed after Mint Superintendent John H. Landis felt the issues were inferior to another model presented by Augustus Saint-Gaudens.

The coin is an important addition to any highly acclaimed collection of Indian Head Eagles.

Few of these coins exist today and its rarity may be especially understated with a seemingly high number of coins having been resubmitted to NGC and PCGS. Using what numbers we have, however, the issue ranks right in the middle of the entire series in terms of its rarity in Gem Uncirculated and finer grades.

Six examples can be found in MS67 by NGC and PCGS combined according to March 2010 population reports.

The surfaces are seen with a few swirling die polish marks but these are found to a much lesser extent than with the earlier Wire Rim version.

Unlike the Wire Rim edition that preceded it, the 1907 Rolled Edge is typically seen with a bright, satiny mint luster.

They are most often weakly struck and lack the level of detail that was present on the Wire Rim coins, especially in the central hair details and in the eagle's wing feathers.

Most coins have a bright yellow-gold color but many can be found with a sunset-like reddish overlay.

There is a single Proof known of this variety. It is not known exactly why it was minted but it was likely a trial piece that has been remarkably preserved after over the past century.

The 1907 Rolled Edge is a legendary rarity, which is considered as one of the true "trophy coins" among 20th century United States gold issues. It is widely believed that only 50 or so of the coins originally struck were spared from the melting pot and most of these are known today. The typical survivor grades MS64 to MS65 and a few superb Gems are known to exist.

1907

No Motto

Mint Engraver Charles Barber used the Saint Gaudens design and inspiration to ultimately come up with this design. It is the third and final Indian Head Eagle dated 1907 and it became the regular issue after the U.S. Mint feared the public might be unhappy with the earlier Rolled Edge version.

Mintage: **239,406**

Overall Rarity: **28 of 32**

Uncirculated Rarity:

MS-62	27 of 32
MS-63	28 of 32
MS-64	30 of 32
MS-65	30 of 32

The periods of this design were removed and the branch below the eagle on the reverse has a different shape. The central hair on the obverse and the feathers on the reverse are typically weaker than later issues but the ends of the feathers were strengthened.

It is a first- year issue and is among the most beautiful coins ever struck by the U.S. Mint. As a result, many examples were saved by collectors and the issue is relatively easy to find in most grades up to Gem Uncirculated and higher. Three pieces have attained an MS68 grade as of March 2010 by PCGS and NGC combined.

There are two Proofs known from this issue. The first issue is a Roman Finish Proof struck in a higher relief than the second, which is in a Matte Proof finish. Both were likely struck on a medal press and were used to present Mint Authorities with what the new design was to look like under the implementation of a properly operated Janvier Reduction machine.

This issue is known for being very well produced with sharp detail seen in the central portions of Liberty's headdress and the peripheral stars. There is also further pronounced definition in the higher parts of the eagle's wing.

Most can be found with deep, satiny luster and an occasional few have also been seen with frosted devices.

The coloration is generally yellow-gold but many show strong hues of green-gold, orange-gold or a rarer reddish-gold.

Eye appeal is outstanding on high-grade specimens but since this date can be found all over the grading spectrum they are most often shown with heavy abrasions that detract from the overall aesthetic properties of the coin.

Augustus Saint Gaudens died on August 3, 1907 and never lived to see his creation actually go into public hands. His legacy, however, is still very much alive today in this breathtaking series of Indian Head Eagles.

This issue, which is most often called the 1907 No Motto by collectors, is relatively common in all grades up to and including MS64. Gems are scarce but are still among the most frequently seen in the Indian Head Eagle series. There are a number of superb pieces available to collectors and with some patience the collector may be able to find a piece which grades MS66 or even MS67.

1908
No Motto

This 1908 No Motto issue is much scarcer than its 1907 predecessor and it has the second lowest mintage of any regular issue in the series. It can be found in Gem grades and although it is certainly outranked by several other challenging dates at this level, it is still quite scarce.

Mintage: 33,500

Overall Rarity: 16 of 32

Uncirculated Rarity:

MS-62	16 of 32
MS-63	18 of 32
MS-64	18 of 32
MS-65	19 of 32

Several carefully preserved and ultra high grade examples as high as MS67 have been seen at auction over the past several years. One coin has achieved an acclaimed MS68 grade and it is housed in an NGC holder.

The strike is generally very strong but we some specimens lack detail in the portions nearest the TY in LIBERTY. A number also show some softness in the eagle's feathers.

Natural coloration is most often a light, apricot-gold hue. Some can be found with a greenish-gold tint and a small number have traces of pink and lilac.

Luster is most often very frosty but there are a moderate number that are seen with a somewhat subdued appearance. An occasional few can be found with a matte-like appearance.

There are a great many 1908 No Motto eagles that can be found with stellar surfaces that appear as though they were pulled right from the dies. However, as this issue can be found all over the grading spectrum it also has its fair share of bagmarks and abrasions.

Since this issue is typically well produced, it is often seen with good eye appeal. Finding a true Gem, however, is another story and properly graded MS65 and better pieces are truly rare.

The 1908 With Motto Eagle is a somewhat common coin from the standpoint of overall rarity. It is fairly relatively easy to locate in circulated grades and in Uncirculated up to the MS62 to MS63 range. It is scarce in MS64 and rarer than generally recognized in MS65. A very small number of MS66 and better coins exist but these are almost never offered for sale.

1908-D

No Motto

The 1908-D No Motto issue is just about as rare overall as its Philadelphia Mint counterpart, despite possessing a much larger mintage. This is due mostly to a lack of continued interest in the novelty of the new design and as a result very few were actually saved.

Mintage: 210,000

Overall Rarity: 15 of 32

Uncirculated Rarity:

MS-62	19 of 32
MS-63	14 of 32
MS-64	10 of 32
MS-65	8 of 32

Most are seen with subdued luster and weaker strikes. They typically lack detail in the hair around Liberty's face and in the feathers on the eagle's shoulder.

The 1908-D No Motto is difficult to find in MS65 and higher grades because strike and luster are two important factors required by the grading services to attain that status. It easily ranks in the top third in the series for high grade coins at the MS65 level and higher. The Finest Known examples include just three MS67's graded by NGC as of March 2010.

This issue is usually regarded as one of the least attractive in the series because of a very flat strike. Softness in the curls of Liberty's hair is considered normal and the coin is generally very weak through the central portions.

Most examples of this date display a satin-like finish but a select few examples are seen with heavily frosted devices. A level of granularity is present on all 1908-D No Motto Eagles.

Luster is well below average for the issue and lacks the vibrancy that many other dates in the series possess. An occasional piece can be obtained with an uncommon presence of brightness and flash. Such coins are considered very desirable by specialists in the series.

Natural coloration is most often a lifeless yellow-gold but some noteworthy examples display rich reddish tinges.

The 1908-D No Motto is only a bit scarcer than the 1908 No Motto in terms of overall rarity but it is much scarcer in high grades. The 1908-D No Motto is most frequently seen in AU55 to MS62 grades. It is scarce in MS63, very scarce in MS64 and very rare in MS65.

Mintmark is above left tip of branch on the 1908-D No Motto, and at left of arrow points thereafter.

Business Strike

Proof

1908
With Motto

The 1908 issue represents
the first in the series to display
the motto IN GOD WE TRUST.
The motto was first placed on
our nation's coinage during
the Civil War.

Mintage: 341,370 + 116 Proofs

Overall Rarity: 24 of 32

Uncirculated Rarity:

MS-62	24 of 32
MS-63	24 of 32
MS-64	22 of 32
MS-65	25 of 32

President Theodore Roosevelt did not like the idea of displaying the name of God on our nation's coinage but Congress went with the demands of the public. Despite Roosevelt's disapproval Congress decided to evoke the authority to tell the Mint to put the motto back on. IN GOD WE TRUST was thus placed prominently next to the Eagle's breast and has never been interrupted on any coin since.

The 1908 With Motto Eagle is usually found with satiny mint luster. A full, sharp strike is typical for this date and this is a reason why a few examples can be found in MS65 and higher grades.

Color is most often a rich yellow-gold but some can be found with heavy hints of apricot-orange. A few are noted with traces of reddish-gold especially prominent in the Indian's headdress.

There were 116 Proofs minted and they can be found in two finishes. The most common is a dark Matte Proof and nearly all known Proofs were struck as such. There is one known Roman or Satin Finish Proof that is believed to have been struck later in the year.

The 1908 With Motto Eagle is relatively easy to locate in circulated grades and it can be found in MS60 to MS63 grades without tremendous effort. It is somewhat scarce in MS64 but it becomes very scarce in MS65. More superb pieces (MS66 and better) examples are known than one might imagine and this may be the result of a small hoard existing at one time. Proofs are very rare with around 40-50 pieces known, mostly in the PR64 to PR66 range.

1908-D
With Motto

This is the first With Motto variety struck at the Denver Mint. The high mintage figure suggests that this is a common issue but it is not. It appears that many were melted and, today, this issue is scarce in all grades. The 1908-D With Motto is actually rarer than the 1908 No Motto, 1908-D No Motto and the 1908 Motto and is extremely difficult to obtain in Gem Uncirculated grades.

Mintage: 836,500

Overall Rarity: 9 of 32

Uncirculated Rarity:

MS-62	13 of 32
MS-63	12 of 32
MS-64	7 of 32
MS-65	10 of 32

Although most examples display a bold strike and booming luster, few have actually survived with the mark-free surfaces that are essential for a coin graded MS65 or higher.

The 1908-D With Motto is usually very well struck with sharp design elements but some are found with a slightly softer strike than would be considered normal for the date.

Although grades higher than MS64 are quite rare, they can be sometimes obtained by the serious collector who is patient and well-funded. Coins which grade as high as MS68 have made appearances at auction in the past several years.

Most 1908-D With Motto Eagles exhibit satiny mint luster that can be categorized as above- average to excellent.

Some are seen with a fine-grain texture in the fields but because a large number of heavily abraded coins exist, this issue is generally perceived as one of the less attractive dates in the series.

The color is most notably an orange-gold but some pieces show hints of lime-green.

The 1908-D With Motto is clearly one of the most underrated dates in the entire Indian Head Eagle series. It is far scarcer than its high original mintage figure would indicate and this is likely explained by a significant number of coins having been melted. Most are seen in the AU55 to MS63 range. Examples grading MS64 to MS65 are extremely scarce. There are a small number of truly exceptional pieces known including two which have been graded MS68 by PCGS.

1908-S

The 1908-S Eagle is popular due to its status as the first coin of this design to have been struck at the San Francisco Mint. It is one of the most aesthetically appealing in the series due to its excellent quality of manufacture.

Mintage: 59,850

Overall Rarity: 11 of 32

Uncirculated Rarity:

MS-62	8 of 32
MS-63	9 of 32
MS-64	11 of 32
MS-65	14 of 32

The date was largely spared from circulation and it is the 18th most common in the series in Gem. Coins as high as MS68 can sometimes be purchased and there is a single, near-perfect MS69 example that NGC has graded. This lone 1908-S MS69 represents one of only two coins in the entire Indian Head Eagle series to ever achieve that stellar level, the other being a single 1907 Wire Rim.

The 1908-S nearly always comes sharply struck with incredible definition in the headdress and in Liberty's hair. Some examples exhibit a light softness at the highest areas of the eagle's feathers on the reverse.

The coin is generally seen in two different finishes. One is extremely satiny while the other is fine and grainy. Both are popular with collectors.

On satin finish examples the luster is extremely vibrant but on granular examples, as would be expected, the luster is less vivid.

The color differs between light orange-gold to greenish-gold or even deep coppery gold.

The eye appeal of the 1908-S is as high as for any date in the Indian Head series. There are a number of pieces available which are fully struck, extremely lustrous and superbly toned. These pieces would make great type coins for the collector seeking a single superb example of this magnificent design.

The 1908-S is actually more available than one might expect. It is seen in grades all the way down to VF and EF, proving that it saw a good deal of circulation. It is relatively easy to locate in AU55 to MS62 but it becomes scarce in MS63 and MS64. Gems are rare but are actually more plentiful than nearly any other San Francisco issue of this type. There are a small number of truly superb pieces in existence including a few that grade as high as MS68 to MS69.

Business Strike

Proof

1909

The 1909 date is one of
the scarcest Philadelphia Mint
issues and it ranks behind only
the rare and very expensive 1933,
1907 Wire Edge and
1907 Rolled Edge varieties.

Mintage: 184,789 + 74 Proofs

Overall Rarity: 20 of 32

Uncirculated Rarity:

MS-62	20 of 32
MS-63	20 of 32
MS-64	17 of 32
MS-65	18 of 32

The 1909 is usually seen with a very sharp strike, as are most Philadelphia issues from this era.

The surfaces are often heavily bagmarked. It appears that the majority of 1909 Eagles that were not melted went into circulation and were roughly handled. It is extremely hard to find a piece which is clean and choice.

The luster is usually very good with a rich satiny texture most often seen. The color is a vibrant yellow-gold but some show modest hints of green-gold.

The level of eye appeal for the 1909 tends to be lower than for the other Philadelphia issues of this era. Many have a "scuffy" appearance which tends to dull the remaining luster. An attractive, high end coin represents an excellent purchase for the savvy collector and many specialists feel that this issue is undervalued at current levels.

There were just 74 Proofs struck and most are seen in a lighter Roman or Satin finish. Two dark Matte Proofs are believed to exist as well. An estimated 30-35 Proofs are known to exist with most of these in the PR64 to PR65 range. In Gem Proof, this issue is exceedingly rare.

The 1909 is considerably scarcer than the 1910-1915 Philadelphia issues. It is usually seen in AU55 to MS63 grades. It is scarce and much underrated in MS64 and properly graded MS65 pieces are very rare. There are a few superb MS66 examples known but these tend to be in strong hands and are seldom offered for sale. The 1909 will prove to be a challenging issue for the collector who is seeking to assemble a very high quality set of Indian Head Eagles.

1909-D

Unless you are a specialist in the series, it is surprising to learn just how scarce this date really is. Despite its relatively high mintage figure of 121,540, the 1909-D is a tough coin in any grade above MS63 and many experts regard it as one of the most undervalued Indian Head Eagles.

Mintage: 121,540

Overall Rarity: 18 of 32

Uncirculated Rarity:
MS-62   17 of 32
MS-63   17 of 32
MS-64   12 of 32
MS-65   5 of 32

The 1909-D comes sharply struck in most respects but the eagle's feathers are typically less well defined than in the other Denver Mint issues.

Luster is most often only average or just slightly better than average atop frosty, finely granular surfaces. Highly lustrous 1909-D Eagles are very uncommon but do exist. Some satiny examples are known but these are not often encountered.

The color is most often a light orange or coppery gold with select greenish highlights.

The level of eye appeal for this date is below average. While most examples are seen with acceptable detail, the typical 1909-D is somewhat dull, and very noticeably abraded. The 1909-D is sometimes lumped together with the very common 1910-D but this is not the case as the 1909-D is considerably scarcer.

The 1909-D is usually found in AU55 to MS63 grades. It is quite scarce in MS64 and it is legitimately rare in properly graded MS65. There are a few pieces known in MS66 but anything higher than this is almost impossible to locate.

1909-S

Before 1977, this issue was nearly impossible to find in Uncirculated condition but an accumulation of about 60 nice Uncirculated pieces was discovered. Despite this find, it is still much harder to obtain than is usually perceived.

It ranks a strong 8th in overall rarity and is certainly within the top half of the series for condition rarity. There is a lone MS68 graded by NGC and both services combined have graded a mere three MS67 coins.

Mintage: **292,350**

Overall Rarity: **8 of 32**

Uncirculated Rarity:

MS-62	11 of 32
MS-63	10 of 32
MS-64	16 of 32
MS-65	13 of 32

The 1909-S issue, like the 1908-S before it, usually exhibits a very sharp strike with good central detail, especially on the obverse.

The natural coloration of this second year San Francisco Mint issue is typically a highly desirable greenish-gold with hints of rose. A few are found with the vibrant yellow-gold color that is most often associated with Philadelphia Mint issues.

The luster varies from coin to coin. Many are found with slightly grainy surfaces while a smaller number are satiny with a more frosty texture.

The 1908-S tends to be a more highly acclaimed coin due to its status as the first Indian Head Eagle from this Mint. The 1909-S is, however, a scarcer coin in terms of overall rarity and it is probably a harder coin to find in Gem condition as well.

The 1909-S is less often found in lower grades than the 1908-S and this is an indication that it did not circulate as readily. It is usually seen in AU55 to MS63 grades. The 1909-S is scarce in MS64 and rare in MS65 although a hoard which was discovered in 1977 has made Gems more available than in the past.

Business Strike

Proof

1910

Despite a relatively small mintage for a Philadelphia Mint issue, the 1910 is actually one of the easiest dates to obtain in all grades thanks to a large number having been saved. In fact, more than 4,000 1910 Eagles have been graded between MS60 and MS64. There are a number of MS66 examples and three MS68's share Finest Known status at NGC; PCGS has graded just three pieces in MS67 with none better.

Mintage: 318,500 + 204 Proofs

Overall Rarity: 25 of 32

Uncirculated Rarity:

MS-62	26 of 32
MS-63	27 of 32
MS-64	25 of 32
MS-65	27 of 32

The luster is seen with less vibrancy than is typical for a Philadelphia minted Indian Head Eagle. It varies from average quality to outstanding on some high quality pieces.

Almost all 1910 Eagles display frosted surfaces with a fine granularity that is typical for a Philadelphia coin. Some can be found with a satin sheen and finding one of these should present a nice challenge for the collector who appreciates this "look."

The frosted, granular specimens exhibit mostly orange and greenish-gold colors, while the less frequently seen satin surface coins display a soft yellow-gold hue.

As this is one of the easier to locate Indian Eagles in all grades, it presents even the novice collector an outstanding opportunity to purchase a really nice, pristine Gem that will not break the bank to acquire.

There were 204 Proofs struck, all with a Roman Finish and unlike the regular issue struck for this date, very few were actually saved. The 1910 is actually one of the most difficult Proofs to obtain and it is doubtful if more than 25 to 30 pieces are known.

The 1910 is one of the more available Indian Head Eagles. It is readily available in grades up to and including MS64. Pieces that grade MS65 are actually a bit scarcer than generally realized although they do not yet bring a significant premium above more common issues like the 1911. In any grade above MS65, the 1910 is quite rare. Proofs are much rarer than their mintage figure of 204 would suggest.

1910-D

The 1910-D is the most common branch mint issue Indian Eagle. Although the date displays a high mintage that actually eclipses the more common 1926, far more of them were melted. Many of them were still saved both in America and abroad and there are a number that are exceptionally well preserved. The date is widely available in all grades up to MS64.

Mintage: 2,356,640

Overall Rarity: 30 of 32

Uncirculated Rarity:

MS-62	30 of 32
MS-63	30 of 32
MS-64	29 of 32
MS-65	29 of 32

It is typical for this issue to display weakened definition in the date, on the stars and the lettering on the reverse. This is likely a result of how the coins were positioned in the collar or because of excessive die wear which is not generally seen in other issues. A fair number are found without these characteristics, however, and can be classified with exceptional strikes. Still, nearly all present plenty of detail on the headdress and on the eagle's wing feathers.

Most 1910-D Eagles are found with satin-like luster that is mostly vibrant and superior for a Denver Mint coin. Usually 1910-D's exhibit moderate orange-gold hues but there are some with a greenish-gold tinge.

The eye appeal is generally high but a large number of heavily abraded coins exist. There is an equal number of genuinely attractive coins with good color, nice luster and a pleasing overall look.

There are 8 MS67's known in NGC holders while PCGS has graded one example this high. There are quite a few MS66 specimens that can be obtained.

The 1910-D is the most common Indian Head Eagle produced at one of the branch mints. It is easily located in grades up to and including MS64. In Gem Uncirculated, it is much harder to find than the 1926 or 1932 issues. Examples which grade MS66 are sometimes available but these are very scarce and pieces in MS67 are very rare, as one might expect.

1910-S

The 1910-S was produced in large quantity and it has the highest mintage figure of all San Francisco Mint Indian Head Eagles. This mintage is deceiving as nearly all were melted during the 1930's and just a few thousand actually still remain today.

Mintage: 811,000

Overall Rarity: 19 of 32

Uncirculated Rarity:

MS-62	18 of 32
MS-63	16 of 32
MS-64	9 of 32
MS-65	4 of 32

Finding this coin in circulated grades is relatively easy and Uncirculated pieces up to MS63 are available. Once higher examples are desired, this date becomes extremely elusive and ranks as the fourth most conditionally challenging coin of the series. In Gem Uncirculated grades and finer this issue becomes extremely rare. NGC and PCGS report a mere five MS66's combined and even fewer MS65's. It is a substantial conditional rarity at this level and it is an issue that, in MS65 or above, is lacking from most collections of Indian Head Eagles.

The 1910-S is ranked at nineteenth in terms of overall rarity because of the number of coins that were disbursed into circulation.

The strike is typically seen with a little bit of weakness underneath the neck of Liberty especially on the digits "1" and "9" in the date. The rest of the date tends to be much sharper than this.

As with many other Indian Head Eagles, the 1910-S is found mostly with frosty surfaces but there are some that have a rich satin appearance. Most are seen with the normal granular look.

The coloration is usually a light orange or faint coppery-gold. There are also a number of rose-gold specimens that can be obtained.

The few relatively high grade pieces which exist tend to have excellent overall eye appeal with great color, surfaces and luster. But most 1910-S Eagles have below average eye appeal on account of abraded surfaces, some weakness of strike and rough handling.

The 1910-S is one of the most unusual dates in the series and it is certainly among the true Condition Rarities of all 20th century United States gold coins. It is reasonably common in circulated grades and can be found in the MS60 to MS62 range without a great effort. It becomes very scarce in properly graded MS63 and MS64 pieces are rare. Gem 1910-S Eagles are exceptionally rare.

1911

Business Strike

Proof

The 1911 issue is the
third most common Philadelphia
Indian Head Eagle, trailing
only the ultra-common
1926 and 1932 dates.

Mintage: 505,500 + 95 Proofs

Overall Rarity: 29 of 32

Uncirculated Rarity:

MS-62	29 of 32
MS-63	29 of 32
MS-64	28 of 32
MS-65	28 of 32

Many Philadelphia Mint Indian Head Eagles were exported to Europe until well after Franklin Roosevelt ordered most gold to be melted down in 1933. This contributes to a large number of coins that can still be found in all grades, including three MS68's that hold the top spot at NGC as of March 2010.

A few decades ago, the 1911 Eagle was regarded as a scarcer coin than it is today. A number of small groups of very high quality pieces have been located in the past two decades and this has made Gem examples far more available to current collectors than in the past.

This issue is normally well struck and most pieces are found with the typical granular, frosty surfaces that are seen on nearly every other Philadelphia Mint Eagle. Some are seen with the satiny texture that is found on other dates. The quality of luster on the 1911 is among the best on any of the Philadelphia issues from this decade.

The coloration is most often a rich orange-gold. Some are found with strong hints of green-gold, while others display a bright, greenish-yellow hue.

The level of eye appeal for this date tends to be among the best in the entire series. With just a bit of patience, the collector should be able to find a really pretty 1911 Eagle which is well struck, very lustrous and attractively toned in natural hues.

There were just 95 Proofs minted in 1911 and an estimated 25-30 pieces are known today. Proof 1911 Eagles are seen with two types of finish: dark matte and sandblast.

The 1911 is among the more common Indian Head Eagles. It is relatively easy to locate in Uncirculated grades up to MS64. Gem Uncirculated pieces are moderately scarce but they are offered for sale with a good degree of frequency. In MS66 and MS67, the 1911 is quite rare. Proofs are very rare with most survivors in the PR64 to PR66 range.

1911-D

The 1911-D is the most conditionally challenging coin in the series. There are only three coins graded MS65 or finer by PCGS and NGC has never awarded this issue a grade of Gem or better. Fewer than 300 examples can be found today in any Mint State grade and most of these are in the MS60 to MS61 range.

Mintage: **30,100**

Overall Rarity: **10 of 32**

Uncirculated Rarity:

MS-62	10 of 32
MS-63	7 of 32
MS-64	4 of 32
MS-65	2 of 32

The 1911-D is generally a well struck issue. On most coins, the obverse is nearly completely defined although there may be a bit of weakness on the curls above the ear of the Indian. The reverse is not as well struck with weakness almost always seen at the center with a resultant loss of detail on the wing feathers near the eagle's breast and the leg feathers below.

The luster on the few higher grade 1911-D Eagles which exist is excellent with a satiny, slightly granular texture noted. Most pieces are worn to the point that their luster is impaired.

As is often the case with Indian Head Eagles, the color is found in orange-gold hues and to a lesser extent with rose and greenish tinges.

The eye appeal is generally below average for the date because of the excessively low quantities that exist in Mint State grades. The 1911-D saw wide circulation and this is clearly evident based on the appearance of the survivors. Aesthetically pleasing coins always command substantial premiums and are the most coveted coins in the entire series.

The 1911-D is the premier condition rarity in the Indian Head Eagle series. It is generally seen in circulated grades and it is scarce in the lower Uncirculated grades. It becomes rare in MS62 and it is very rare in properly graded MS63. In MS64 and MS65, the 1911-D is extremely rare.

1911-S

Prior to the 1970's it was thought that the 1911-S was similar in rarity to the 1911-D but a small hoard of approximately 30 to 40 very high quality pieces found in Europe changed that notion.

Mintage: **51,000**

Overall Rarity: **6 of 32**

Uncirculated Rarity:

MS-62	6 of 32
MS-63	4 of 32
MS-64	8 of 32
MS-65	17 of 32

Today the issue is still very scarce overall with probably fewer than 550 coins known in all grades. Although a moderate number of Gem Uncirculated coins exists (perhaps as many as two dozen), there have been none graded finer than MS66. A vast majority of the 550 or so presently known are in grades of EF to AU.

Almost all 1911-S Eagles are found with sharp strikes. The detail is uncommonly sharp at the centers for a coin of this design from the San Francisco Mint and a number are seen with partial wire rims as well.

The luster is usually seen bright with frosted finishes atop the normal finely granular surfaces.

The color is the regular orange-gold from San Francisco with many displaying strong hints of dark green. A few Gem examples exhibit deep reddish-gold accents.

The eye appeal of this date tends to be below average. Most 1911-S Eagles are heavily abraded and have substandard luster as a result. Locating a very attractive specimen is difficult and coins with good eye appeal routinely trade for strong premiums among knowledgeable specialists.

The fact that there was a decent sized hoard of Gem 1911-S Eagles at one time should not deter the advanced collector from according this date a high level of respect. These coins have been long since dispersed and, today, no more than one or two Gems are seen at auction on an annual basis.

The 1911-S is among the scarcer dates in this series from the standpoint of overall rarity. It is sometime seen in Uncirculated and the typical Mint State coin is in the MS62 to MS63 range. The 1911-S is very scarce in MS64 and rare in MS65. PCGS has graded nine examples of this date in MS66 with none better but it is unlikely that this many superb pieces actually exist.

Business Strike

Proof

1912

Most Philadelphia Mint issues fall in the lower tier in terms of overall rarity and this date is no exception. High grade examples of the 1912 are noticeably harder to find than the 1908 With Motto, the 1910 and the 1911.

Mintage: 405,000 + 83 Proofs

Overall Rarity: 27 of 32

Uncirculated Rarity:
- MS-62   28 of 32
- MS-63   26 of 32
- MS-64   24 of 32
- MS-65   23 of 32

In 1912, the Eagle saw a subtle but important addition to the design. The edge had two additional stars placed on it to represent the addition of New Mexico and Arizona to the Union, bringing the total number of stars from 46 to 48.

The 1912 is usually seen with a razor sharp strike with extremely good detail on the obverse. On some pieces, the reverse is not as well struck with some minor weakness on the eagle's front leg and the breast feathers.

Granularity is present on this issue, as it is with all Philadelphia Eagles but it is displayed to a lesser extent on the 1912 than it is on the previous 1911.

Some 1912 Eagles are seen with bright, frosty luster while the majority are slightly dull with a grainy texture. The color is usually a medium to deep yellow-gold with an occasional green-gold or coppery-gold piece to be found.

The eye appeal is generally very good on this issue and outstanding examples are often made available to collectors.

All Proof 1912 Eagles are seen with a dark matte finish which is unique to this year. A total of 83 Proofs were struck but a number of these were melted and survivors are very rare. An estimated 25-30 are known today with most of these in the PR64 to PR65 range. A few superb pieces are known including some that grade as high as PR67 or even PR68.

The 1912 is a moderately scarce and decidedly undervalued issue that is not hard to find in the AU to MS63 grades. It is moderately scarce in MS64 and it is scarce in MS65. Examples that grade MS66 are very rare and there are just a small number of pieces known that grade MS67.

1912-S

The 1912-S is a true condition rarity in the Indian Head Eagle series. Nearly every known piece is very poorly struck with a considerable lack of detail, even less than the 1911-S and 1913-S.

Mintage: **300,000**

Overall Rarity: 14 of 32

Uncirculated Rarity:

MS-62   12 of 32
MS-63   13 of 32
MS-64   14 of 32
MS-65   9 of 32

Due to this particularly weak strike and lack of detail, the 1912-S is very difficult to find in MS64 and higher grades. At the MS66 level the coin is exceptionally rare, with NGC reporting as of March 2010 that just two have been graded that high with none higher. PCGS reports just a single MS66 graded, also with none seen higher.

In terms of overall rarity the 1912-S ranks near the middle of the series with a relatively high mintage for a San Francisco Mint issue with 300,000 struck. The date sees an even mixture between circulated grades and Uncirculated grades, with the Uncirculated grades up to near Gem quality only slightly harder to locate. The highest concentration of Uncirculated specimens lie at the MS62 level and probably fewer than 100 examples are known in properly graded MS63 or better.

The strike on the 1912-S is below average and a significant lack of detail is seen in the hair around the face, with special concentration at the RTY in LIBERTY. A significant loss of detail can also often be seen on the eagle's shoulder on the reverse.

The luster is well below average for this date, probably a result also of its weak strike and most examples come very dull in appearance. The surfaces are always found with a frosty texture accentuated by an above average level of granularity.

The color on the 1912-S Eagle is usually a faint peach-orange or sometimes greenish-gold. Many have been cleaned or dipped and do not show natural coloration as a result.

Because of the dull luster and very weak strike that is most often seen with this date it would be considered near the bottom of the series in terms of overall eye appeal. Nice examples are quite rare and when a high quality piece with good eye appeal is offered for sale, it typically brings well over current catalog valuation.

The 1912-S is most often seen in AU50 to MS60 grades. It is scarce in the lower Uncirculated grades and it becomes rare in MS63. It is very rare in MS64 and extremely rare in MS65.

Business Strike

Proof

1913

As is the case with every other Philadelphia Mint Eagle, the 1913 is considered a common issue with a mintage of 442,000 and it can be obtained at all levels up to Gem Uncirculated (MS65). Once better than Gem examples are desired, however, the coin becomes quite elusive. Surprisingly, there is but a single MS67 example graded by PCGS with none higher and NGC has seen none higher than MS66 as of March 2010.

Mintage: 442,000 + 71 Proofs

Overall Rarity: 26 of 32

Uncirculated Rarity:

MS-62	25 of 32
MS-63	26 of 32
MS-64	26 of 32
MS-65	24 of 3

The lone PCGS MS67 example noted above came out of hiding in 2006. The few MS66 examples which have been available to collectors have also brought strong prices.

It should be noted that an accumulation of high grade examples has hit the market in recent years. This accumulation has likely done little to alter the coin's conditional rarity but it is still worthy of mention.

The 1913 Eagle is almost always highly lustrous, as are most other Philadelphia Mint Eagles but this issue has among the best luster of any coin in the series and, as such, it is popular with type collectors.

The strike on these coins is superb and all details can be seen in exceptionally sharp clarity.

The color is often seen in a greenish-gold hue or sunny yellow-gold. The surfaces are most often seen frosty or satiny in appearance. As mentioned above, this date is popular with type collectors due to the fact that some really attractive pieces are available with great color and luster.

There were just 71 Proofs minted in 1913, all with the fine sandblast finish that was used in 1912 as well. This is among the rarest Proofs of this design and it is likely that no more than 20-25 pieces exist. These are typically seen in the PR64 to PR66 range.

The 1913 is a scarcer issue than the 1910, 1911 and 1912 but it is more available than the 1914 and the 1915. It is common in circulated grades and easy to locate in MS63 and even MS64. It is scarce and under appreciated in MS65 and it is quite rare in MS66.

1913-S

For many years, the 1913-S was believed to be the rarest Indian Head Eagle in Gem Uncirculated. Third-party grading has shown that this honor belongs to the 1911-D but the 1913-S is still an exceedingly rare coin in MS65 which creates considerable interest whenever it appears for sale. Just six have been graded at the MS65 level or better.

Mintage: **66,000**

Overall Rarity: 12 of 32

Uncirculated Rarity:

MS-62	7 of 32
MS-63	5 of 32
MS-64	5 of 32
MS-65	3 of 32

NGC reports that two MS67's have been graded with none higher and PCGS reports a single MS66 with none higher.

This date overall ranks in the top third of all Indian Eagles but should still be considered very, very scarce in any grade. Most known examples seen today fall between heavily circulated VF to lightly circulated AU. Uncirculated examples are scarce in any grade and even in the near Gem condition of MS64 there are just twenty-five examples graded by NGC and PCGS combined.

The 1913-S usually comes very boldly struck, unlike the 1912-S that preceded it, and enhanced definition can be seen throughout. Like the 1911-S, this issue shows a partial rim exhibited on the obverse of the coin.

The luster on this issue, while noticeably better than the 12-S, is moderately subdued when compared to the other coins in the series.

The eye appeal on this issue tends to be well below average. The typical example has been roughly handled and shows numerous scuffmarks on the surfaces which affect the luster and color as well. The few known high quality 1913-S Eagles are extremely attractive, so nice pieces are available, albeit for a heavy price.

The 1913-S Eagle is regarded as one of the great condition rarities in all of the 20th century US gold series. It is moderately scarce even in circulated grades and the small numbers of Uncirculated pieces that exist consist mainly of MS60 to MS62 pieces. In MS63, this date is rare and it is very rare in MS64.

1914

Business Strike

Proof

Although generally perceived
as another common
Philadelphia Mint issue,
the 1914 is scarcer
than generally believed.

Mintage: 151,000 + 50 Proofs

Overall Rarity: 21 of 32

Uncirculated Rarity:

    MS-62   21 of 32
    MS-63   22 of 32
    MS-64   21 of 32
    MS-65   21 of 32

This date is displays the typical granular, matte-like surfaces that are so normal for the series. The 1914 is also noted with more mint frost than is usually seen for a Philadelphia issue of this design.

The strike is as sharp as on most any other Philadelphia Indian Eagle and all design elements can be seen with remarkable clarity. The luster typically exhibits a great deal of "flash," as can be expected from a coin with this amount of mint frost.

Because the 1914 Eagle is harder to obtain in Mint State than most other Indian Eagles from this mint, it typically comes very heavily abraded and bagmarked. However, nice examples that were saved during World War I can sometimes be had for a price.

There are only three coins graded MS67 by PCGS and NGC combined as of March 2010 and those three represent the Finest Known examples.

Many specialists in the series feel that the 1914 is an undervalued issue that could become more expensive to add to your collection in the future.

There were a mere 50 Proofs minted in 1914 and this is the rarest Proof in the series. There are, at most, twenty or so examples known with most of these in the PR64 to PR66 range. A few superb Gems are known and these are very rare.

The 1914 is an undervalued issue which is much scarcer than generally believed. It can be found in grades up to and including MS63 without much of an effort but it becomes scarce in MS64 and it is rare in MS65. There are eighteen coins known in MS66 to MS67 grades and these are seldom made available to collectors.

1914-D

It is often stated that the 1914-D is the second most common branch mint Indian Head Eagle struck and while this is technically true, it can still hardly be mentioned in the same sentence as the very common 1910-D. Most of the original mintage from this issue was melted down but enough still exist today in most grades to satisfy the demand for the date.

Mintage: 343,500

Overall Rarity: 22 of 32

Uncirculated Rarity:

MS-62	22 of 32
MS-63	21 of 32
MS-64	23 of 32
MS-65	20 of 32

There have been nine total MS67's graded by PCGS and NGC combined as of March 2010.

Unlike other Denver Mint Indian Head Eagles, the 1914-D only suffers from traces of granularity, as opposed to the overall roughness that appears on other issues. The luster is always exceptional with a frosty texture.

The strike is usually sharp and the 1914-D is regarded as among the better detailed Denver issues of this type, making it popular among collectors seeking a single Denver Indian Head Eagle.

The color varies from mostly faint greenish-gold to an attractive reddish-orange hue.

As most examples saw wide circulation this date is plagued with heavy abrasions and generally doesn't come with outstanding eye appeal, though the excellent mint luster often outweighs the typically heavily marked surfaces.

There is an interesting planchet flaw present on many 1914-D Indian Eagles that appears as an indentation on the "19" in the date. This is caused by the minting process and it is not considered to be a significant defect.

The 1914-D can be found with relative ease in grades up to MS64. It is actually quite scarce in MS65 and it is very rare above this.

1914-S

With a mintage of 208,000 the 1914-S seems like just another relatively common date in the series. In actuality, this underrated date just barely misses the top third in grades of MS65 and finer and is rarer than the 1908-S, 1909-S, 1911-S and even the highly collectable 1930-S at Gem. Fewer than 1,200 examples can be found in all grades by the two major grading services combined.

Mintage: **208,000**

Overall Rarity: **17 of 32**

Uncirculated Rarity:

MS-62	14 of 32
MS-63	19 of 32
MS-64	19 of 32
MS-65	12 of 32

The luster is generally very brilliant and superior to that seen on most other issues in the series.

Most examples exhibit a green-gold hue but there are also a number that display fiery coppery highlights. Some show rich overlays of rose and tiny suggestions of orange peel.

The strike is usually fairly sharp but there is often some level of detail missing at the top of the eagle's wing on the reverse.

There is a single NGC MS67 specimen that is the Finest Known. The 1914-S is particularly scarce in MS66 as well, with just four total graded that high by NGC and PCGS combined as of March 2010.

The serious collector of Indian Head Eagles will find the 1914-S to be among the most conditionally challenging in the series and many years may pass before a strict Gem Uncirculated example is made available.

The 1914-S is relatively easy to obtain in circulated grades and is sometimes seen in the lower Uncirculated grades as well. It becomes quite scarce in properly graded MS63 and it is rare in MS64. In MS65, the 1914-S eagle is very rare and it is extremely rare in MS66.

1915

Business Strike

Proof

The 1915 is the final Indian Head Eagle produced at the Philadelphia Mint during the 1910's, which discontinued production of this denomination until 1926. It is a fairly common date that is well-regarded for its aesthetic appeal and popular with type collectors.

Mintage: 351,000 + 75 Proofs

Overall Rarity: 23 of 32

Uncirculated Rarity:

MS-62	23 of 32
MS-63	23 of 32
MS-64	27 of 32
MS-65	26 of 32

This is a very well struck issue which typically has complete detail on the eagle's hair and the eagle's feathers. A few are seen with weakness at the centers but locating a sharply detailed example will prove to be easy for the collector.

Many 1915 Eagles are abraded and this makes Gem Uncirculated examples scarcer than most people realize.

The luster on this issue is excellent with the typical example possessing thick, frosty luster that lacks the grainy textures seen on the branch mint Indian Head Eagles from this era.

Few dates in this series show better coloration than the 1915. It is possible to locate examples with splendid rich natural coloration including deep green-gold, rose or orange-gold hues.

The 1915 is generally seen with excellent eye appeal. Most are well struck and nicely toned with good luster. It can be hard to find a piece which is not heavily abraded.

There were 75 Proofs minted in 1915 with the same coarse finish that was seen on the 1914 examples. This represents the last year that Proofs were minted. An estimated two dozen or so Proofs are known to exist and most are in the PR64 to PR66 range.

The 1915 is a relatively common date which is well-known for its good eye appeal. It is easy to find in grades up to and including MS64 but Gems are not readily available and probably no more than four or five dozen pieces are known. In MS66 and higher grades, the 1915 is rare. The finest graded by PCGS is an MS67; NGC shows four in this grade with none better as of March 2010.

1915-S

The 1915-S has the second lowest mintage of all Indian Eagles struck at the San Francisco Mint and is extremely difficult to locate in Gem Uncirculated grades. It is one of the few coins in the series that is not only very difficult to find in high grades, but is also a challenge to find in just about any grade above AU55.

Mintage: 59,000

Overall Rarity: 7 of 32

Uncirculated Rarity:

MS-62   9 of 32
MS-63   8 of 32
MS-64   6 of 32
MS-65   6 of 32

Unlike some of the other San Francisco Eagles from this decade, no substantial hoards of this date have been found. A few pieces are found from time to time in Europe but these tend to be circulated examples with poor eye appeal.

It has been stated in the past that this is not a well struck issue but this is not true as many 1915-S Eagles are seen with excellent strikes. Most pieces are fully detailed at the centers and may show noticeable wire edges on the rims as well.

Original examples show very attractive reddish-gold and orange-gold color as is typical of the San Francisco issues of this design. As the collector becomes more familiar with Indian Head Eagles, he will quickly be able to distinguish between the San Francisco, Denver and Philadelphia coins based on their color as each of the three mints produced pieces with very different hues.

The luster is satiny and tends to show less graininess than on some of the other early San Francisco issues. Many 1915-S Eagles are extensively abraded and other show dark spots which are not appealing. It is extremely hard to find a piece with clean, vibrant surfaces.

Most 1915-S Eagles have below average eye appeal and this is one of the reasons why this date is so rare in Gem Uncirculated. The typical example is well struck and lustrous but very bagmarked.

The 1915-S is a rare date both from the standpoint of overall availability and rarity in higher grades. It is seen most often in the AU55 to MS62 range and it becomes quite scarce in MS63. MS64 examples of this date are rare and Gems are extremely rare.

1916-S

This is the last year the Eagle was struck before the United States entered into World War I that cost more than 100,000 American lives and more than 8 million lives worldwide. This conflict went on until 1918 and Indian Eagle coinage did not again resume until 1920.

Mintage: 138,500

Overall Rarity: 13 of 32

Uncirculated Rarity:

MS-62	15 of 32
MS-63	15 of 32
MS-64	13 of 32
MS-65	11 of 32

The 1916-S was actually once rarer than it is today. A couple of small hoards were found in the 1970's that brought to light approximately 125 pieces. It is now the tenth most difficult coin to obtain in Gem Uncirculated and finer condition and the thirteenth most difficult in the series overall. The issue didn't see massive circulation, likely because of the public – and the government's – preoccupation with the conflict going on in Europe and increased confidence in paper money after the establishment of the Federal Reserve. The following year actually saw no gold coins struck at all with the U.S. declaration of war on Germany.

Because the 1916-S didn't see circulation the great majority are found in AU and the lower mint state grades. This issue is very hard to find in Gem Uncirculated as the surfaces tend to be very heavily abraded.

Surviving coins usually exhibit a sharp strike but there is often a degree of clarity missing from the eagle's upper wing tip on the reverse. This is common on many coins in the series and should not be severely discounted.

The luster on the 1916-S generally ranges between moderately subdued to bright and flashy. The color ranges from greenish-gold to orange-gold.

The eye appeal of this date is generally somewhat below average. While most are well struck, it is very hard to find a piece that does not show detracting marks. In addition, the luster is not as good as on some of the earlier San Francisco Eagles of this design.

This is the last of the relatively affordable San Francisco Indian Head Eagles and this makes the 1916-S a very popular issue.

The 1916-S saw limited circulation and is usually seen in AU55 to MS62 grades. It becomes noticeably scarce in MS63 and it is rare in MS64. At one time this date was essentially unknown in Gem Uncirculated but the discovery of some small hoards have made the 1916-S more collectible in MS65.

1920-S

The 1920-S is the third rarest Indian Head Eagle from the standpoint of availability in all grades. It is also among the rarest in Uncirculated grades and in Gem Uncirculated and finer grades.

Mintage: 126,500

Overall Rarity: 3 of 32

Uncirculated Rarity:

MS-62	3 of 32
MS-63	3 of 32
MS-64	1 of 32
MS-65	4 of 32

Unlike other rare United States gold issues from the 1920's, the 1920-S Eagle appears to have been used in circulation as more are known in circulated grades than in Mint State. It also appears that a substantial number of these pieces were melted and that the survival rate is among the lowest of any Indian Head Eagle relative to the original mintage figure.

The quality of strike seen on this date is very distinctive. The RTY in LIBERTY is often very weak and on some pieces it is so faint that it is nearly impossible to discern with the naked eye. Many others are weak on the top of the 19 and the bottom of the 2 in the date. A small number of pieces are sharp on the obverse and these are much more desirable than the typical weakly struck 1920-S Eagle. The reverse is always weak on the eagle's wing and the front leg.

Many of the circulated 1920-S Eagles which exist have been roughly handled and show noticeable marks or evidence of cleaning on the surfaces. The Uncirculated pieces tend to be weakly struck (see above) and have a number of handling marks in the fields.

The luster on higher grade examples is generally quite good with a rich, frosty texture seen on a number of coins. A smaller number of coins have a subdued, grainy texture which is not especially attractive. The natural coloration is a medium to deep rose and orange-gold hue.

For the serious date collector, the 1920-S will prove to be one of the hardest Indian Head Eagles to find. Only a few examples are offered for sale each year and the few high grade pieces which exist tend to be placed in private collections and held for a long period of time.

The 1920-S is a scarce coin in all grades and a rare one in Uncirculated. It is most often seen in AU55 to MS61. It is quite rare in the MS62 to MS64 range and it is extremely rare in Gem Uncirculated. In fact, it is doubtful if more than a dozen Gems exist. The finest known is a PCGS MS67.

1926

The 1926 is the second most common Indian Head Eagle, trailing only the ubiquitous 1932. It is easy to locate in all grades up to and including MS65 but it is considerably harder to find than the 1932 in Gem condition.

Mintage: 1,014,000

Overall Rarity: 31 of 32

Uncirculated Rarity:

MS-62	31 of 32
MS-63	31 of 32
MS-64	31 of 32
MS-65	31 of 32

This tends to be a very well struck issue. Most 1926 Eagles are fully detailed at the centers and the borders. On a few pieces, there is some weakness on the curls around the Indian's ear but a sharply struck piece can be found with relatively minimal effort.

The surfaces on many 1926 Eagles show unsightly deep marks which resemble cuts. This is also seen on 1932 Eagles. It appears that these are mint-made and occurred during the minting process. Many 1926 Eagles have copper spots. These are not considered detracting unless they are overly extensive or positioned in a prominent place such as the cheek of the Indian.

The luster on 1926 Eagles ranges from slightly grainy in texture to very frosty. None of these textures is "better" than the other and it is up to the collector to decide which of these is preferable. The coloration ranges greatly as well with pieces known that show rich orange-gold, rose and greenish-gold or more subdued shades.

The eye appeal on 1926 Indian Head Eagles is usually very good and it is easy to find a high quality example which is well struck, lustrous, attractively toned and which shows reasonably unobtrusive marks.

The 1926 Eagle is very common in all grades up to and including MS64. Gems are not rare but they are harder to locate than the 1932. Properly graded MS66 coins are very rare and in MS67 this date appears to be all but unknown.

1930-S

After a ten-year hiatus, production of the Indian Head Eagle resumed at the San Francisco Mint. This is the final mint marked date of this design and it is one of the rarer dates in the series from the standpoint of overall rarity. Unlike the earlier dates from this mint, the 1930-S did not appear to circulate and, as a result, it is almost never seen in grades below MS60.

Mintage: 96,000

Overall Rarity: 4 of 32

Uncirculated Rarity:

MS-62	4 of 32
MS-63	6 of 32
MS-64	15 of 32
MS-65	16 of 32

The 1930-S is much more sharply struck than the 1920-S although some pieces are not fully detailed at the central obverse. Typically, there is some weakness on the curls around the face and on the reverse at the lower portion of the eagle's wing and the nearby leg.

Many 1930-S Eagles were roughly handled and as a result, the surfaces are often heavily abraded. It appears that a few small hoards have been found on which the surfaces are much cleaner and these pieces were probably not thrown loosely into bags as with other surviving examples.

The luster on this issue is excellent with a thick, frosty texture seen on virtually all survivors. The coloration is very distinctive with vivid yellow-gold or green-gold and rose hues. Many 1930-S Eagles have small copper spots and these are not considered detracting unless they are extensive or positioned in a prominent viewing spot.

The eye appeal on this date is very good and nearly every known example shows excellent color and luster. Excessive bagmarks can be a problem with this issue but if a collector is patient, he should be able to find a very good looking piece for his set.

The 1932 Eagle is extremely common in the lower Uncirculated grades and can be found in MS64 and even MS65 without much effort. It becomes very rare in MS66 and it is exceedingly rare in MS67.

1932

The 1932 is, by a large margin, the most common Indian Head Eagle. There are tens of thousands of coins known and a stream of 1932 Eagles are still being found in overseas sources and are being repatriated back to the United States. This date is easily found in any grade up to and including MS65 and it is more available in superb Gem Uncirculated than any other date in this series as well.

Mintage: 4,463,000

Overall Rarity: 32 of 32

Uncirculated Rarity:

MS-62   32 of 32
MS-63   32 of 32
MS-64   32 of 32
MS-65   32 of 32

This is a very well produced issue. The obverse is usually quite well detailed although it is not uncommon for pieces to show slight weakness on the curls below BERT in LIBERTY.

There are at least two interesting tendencies that are found on most 1932 Eagles. On many coins, there are unusual, deep cuts in the surfaces which do not appear to be abrasions. It is possible that these are mint-made. On many other 1932 Eagles, the surfaces are spotted. These spots are not considered detracting if they are light and not prominently positioned but they are felt to have a negative impact on eye appeal if they are too abundant or located on Liberty's face.

The luster is excellent and is probably as good as on any issue in this series. Many pieces have rich, frosty luster which can be extremely attractive. The coloration on many 1932 Eagles is outstanding as well. Pieces are known with a variety of rich natural coloration including green-gold, orange-gold and rich rose-gold hues.

The 1932 Eagle has good eye appeal except for the fact that most examples are seen with deep, detracting cuts at the central obverse and reverse. Any example with good color and luster which does not show these marks is very scarce and extremely desirable.

Because of its availability in higher grades, the 1932 (along with the 1926) tends to be the single most popular date of this design with type collectors.

The 1932 Eagle is extremely common in the lower Uncirculated grades and can be found in MS64 and even MS65 without much effort. It becomes very rare in MS66 and it is exceedingly rare in MS67.

1933

In March 1933,
Franklin D. Roosevelt signed
a law which halted the
production and release of gold
coins. This effectively ended
the production of Eagles,
which had begun in 1795.

Mintage: **312,500**

Overall Rarity: 1 of 32

Uncirculated Rarity:

MS-62   1 of 32
MS-63   2 of 32
MS-64   3 of 32
MS-65   7 of 32

The 1933 Eagle is the only gold coin with this magical date to be considered legal. It is a much rarer coin than its original mintage figure suggests as nearly every piece was melted. At one point it was believed that fewer than two dozen examples were known but this estimate seems to be on the low side and the actual number is more likely somewhere in the area of three to four dozen.

Since this issue did not circulate, it is almost never seen in grades below MS63 to MS64. But Gems are extremely rare.

The 1933 is usually seen with a good strike. The obverse shows a bit of weakness on the curls below BER in LIBERTY and a few pieces have some lightness on the tips of the feathers from 3:00 to 5:00. The reverse is always seen with good detail although the breast feathers are not fully defined.

For some reason, this date is usually seen with scattered deep marks. The typical 1933 may not have as many abrasions as on the typical 1932 but the marks seen on the 1933 are often located in prime focal points and they can be fairly detracting. More often than not, the marks are located on the obverse and on a few pieces they are positioned squarely on the jaw or cheek of the Indian.

The luster is outstanding with a very rich, frosty texture seen on all surviving pieces.

The natural coloration is a medium to deep orange-gold with some greenish-gold undertones. A few pieces have been seen with reddish copper spots on both the obverse and on the reverse.

Due to the rarity of this date, eye appeal is not as great a factor as it is on other Indian Head Eagles. In addition, most 1933 Eagles are attractive coins although some have abrasions which can be considered fairly detracting. Collectors will not have many opportunities to purchase examples of this date, though, so eye appeal does not play as great a role as it does on a Condition Rarity such as the 1913-S.

There is a single NGC MS66 graded that represents the Finest Known as of March 2010.

The 1933 is the rarest Indian Head Eagle in terms of overall rarity. It is a celebrated issue for a number of reasons. It is the only Indian Head gold coin minted in 1933. Ownership of a 1933 is considered one of the highlights of an advanced set of Indian Head Eagles.

$10 INDIAN HEAD EAGLES - CHECK LIST

DATE - MINT	NGC	PCGS	GRADE	SMITHSONIAN*	DATE - ACQUIRED	NOTES
1907 Wire Rim	☐	☐		MS 66		
1907 Rolled Edge	☐	☐		MS 67		
1907 No Motto	☐	☐		MS 69		
1908 No Motto	☐	☐		MS 67		
1908-D No Motto	☐	☐		MS 60		
1908 With Motto	☐	☐		MS 63		
1908-D With Motto	☐	☐		AU Cleaned		
1908-S	☐	☐		AU Cleaned		
1909	☐	☐		AU 50		
1909-D	☐	☐		AU Polished		
1909-S	☐	☐		AU 58		
1910	☐	☐		MS 65		
1910-D	☐	☐		MS 62		
1910-S	☐	☐		MS 60		
1911	☐	☐		MS 62		

* Finest gold coin specimen in the National Numismatic Collection of the Smithsonian Institution

Indian Gold Coins

DATE - MINT	NGC	PCGS	GRADE	SMITHSONIAN* GRADE	DATE - ACQUIRED	NOTES
☐ 1911-D ☐	☐		_____	MS 62		
☐ 1911-S ☐	☐		_____	EF 45		
☐ 1912 ☐	☐		_____	MS 62		
☐ 1912-S ☐	☐		_____	EF 45		
☐ 1913 ☐	☐		_____	MS 64		
☐ 1913-S ☐	☐		_____	AU 58		
☐ 1914 ☐	☐		_____	MS 60		
☐ 1914-D ☐	☐		_____	AU 58		
☐ 1914-S ☐	☐		_____	AU 58		
☐ 1915 ☐	☐		_____	MS 62		
☐ 1915-S ☐	☐		_____	MS 64		
☐ 1916-S ☐	☐		_____	MS 67		
☐ 1920-S ☐	☐		_____	MS 66		
☐ 1926 ☐	☐		_____	MS 65		
☐ 1930-S ☐	☐		_____	MS 67		
☐ 1932 ☐	☐		_____	MS 65		
☐ 1933 ☐	☐		_____	MS 65		

* Finest gold coin specimen in the National Numismatic Collection of the Smithsonian Institution

IDENTITY ⬤ MATTERS

A COIN BY ANY OTHER NAME STILL SHINES AS BRIGHTLY

> "WHAT'S IN A NAME?
> THAT WHICH WE CALL A ROSE BY ANY
> OTHER NAME WOULD SMELL AS SWEET."

Those famous lines were penned by William Shakespeare for Romeo and Juliet, one of his most popular plays. Juliet speaks them in professing her love for Romeo – a love that transcends their families' bitter feud and makes their surnames irrelevant.

The simple yet eloquent words cut to the very core of the poignant drama – a tale retold in modern American terms in West Side Story.

The language of numismatics is far more prosaic. Shakespeare's basic message is universal, though: People or things remain the same – just as beautiful, just as appealing, just as worthy of admiration – no matter what people call them.

In the numismatic world, very different names frequently are used to describe the identical coins.

Learning the various names associated with a given coin can sometimes be much more than just a diverting way to pass the time. Now and then, it can furnish important information on how to identify the coin in price guides and other publications.

William Shakespeare

1918 Illinois Centennial Half Dollar

Consider, for example, the 1918 half dollar issued to celebrate the 100th anniversary of Illinois' admission to the Union. The obverse of this coin carries the portrait of a younger, beardless Abraham Lincoln, the state's most famous son – and, for that reason, it's commonly referred to as the "Lincoln commemorative half."

1918
Illinois Centennial
Half Dollar

But some major price guides list the coin as the "Illinois Centennial" commemorative, while still others label it the "Lincoln-Illinois" half dollar. Someone unfamiliar with these terms might have difficulty looking up the value and other facts and figures about the coin.

The moral is clear: Unless you're aware of all the names by which a coin is known, you might end up looking for that coin in the wrong place. This, then, is one case where it pays to know a "rose" by every name.

Winged Liberty Head Dime

The "Mercury dime," is another example. For nearly a century, that has been the name most commonly applied to the U.S. 10-cent piece designed by Adolph A. Weinman for the new silver coinage of 1916. The

Winged
Liberty Head Dime

name reflects the popular perception that the figure depicted on the obverse of the coin is Mercury, the winged messenger of the gods in Roman mythology.

To Weinman, however, the figure portrayed was Liberty and the wings crowning her cap represented freedom of thought. Thus, more punctilious numismatists – including some writers and editors – insist that the coin should be called the "Winged Liberty Head dime."

Either way, this diminutive masterpiece is just as lovely to behold and just as worthwhile to collect.

Buffalo Nickel

For almost the same length of time, most Americans have used the term "buffalo nickel" to describe the stunning coin designed by James Earle Fraser and

Buffalo Nickel

struck by the U.S. Mint from 1913 to 1938. But some prefer to call it the "Indian Head five-cent piece," focusing on the obverse's American Indian, rather than the animal on the reverse.

To complicate matters, the animal isn't really a buffalo; it's an American bison. But, as Shakespeare said, what's in a name? Whatever it's called, the beast on Fraser's coin is truly majestic.

Some would argue, too, that "Indian" is inappropriate terminology and should be replaced by "Native American." That, of course, would require renaming not only the buffalo nickel but also many other U.S. coins – among them the "Indian Head" Cent, Eagle, Half Eagle and Quarter Eagle.

What would Shakespeare think of such a change?

The Founding Fathers Define The "Eagle"

"Eagle" was the name the Founding Fathers chose for the $10 gold piece, the most prestigious coin – and the one with the highest face value – in the new nation's monetary lineup. They also authorized two smaller gold coins called the Half Eagle and Quarter Eagle, whose weight and face value ($5 and $2.50, respectively) were exactly one-half and one-quarter as much as those of the Eagle.

Appropriately, all three of these coins – plus a later addition, the Double Eagle (or $20 gold piece) – bore designs on the reverse depicting the national bird throughout their production history. Most of them, however, also have come to be known by names based primarily on their obverse portraiture. And one – the Saint-Gaudens Double Eagle – is known by the name of the artist who designed it.

Thus, many hobbyists speak of "Capped Bust" and "Liberty Head" $10's, $5's and $2.50's and "Classic Head" gold coins, using terms that refer to the likeness of Miss Liberty on their obverse. And there are also "Indian Head" coins in all three of these denominations – plus the gold dollar – and an "Indian Princess" $3 gold piece because their obverse portraits were inspired by American Indians.

$10 Indian Eagle

$5 Indian
Half Eagle

$2.5 Indian
Quarter Eagle

A "3-Cent" Piece Was First To Be Called "Nickel"

The term "nickel" is synonymous today with the five-cent piece. Originally, though, ordinary Americans coined the term as a name for the three-cent piece of the same composition when Uncle Sam started minting that coin in 1865.

3 Cent
Silver Piece

The nickel three-cent piece became an immediate hit, prompting Congress to authorize a five-cent nickel coin, which made its first appearance the following year. Within a few years, the three-cent version had fallen out of favor with the public, but the five-cent nickel had taken root as a permanent part of the U.S. coinage lineup.

In both cases, the term "nickel" was somewhat misleading, since both contained three times more copper than nickel (just as the Jefferson nickel does today). But the use of nickel in coinage, even as a "minority partner," was relatively new, having started in America less than a decade earlier in the Flying Eagle cent — so that's what people focused on.

3 Cent
Nickel Piece

It wasn't the name that mattered, however. People embraced the coins because they were useful and convenient — regardless of what they were called.

The Antecedents of the Modern Nickel

The notion of a three-cent piece seems extremely odd today — but the debut of the three-cent nickel actually gave Americans two different coins of that denomination. Since 1851, the U.S. Mint had been making a tiny three-cent piece containing mostly silver.

This coin was known more formally as the "trime," but the general public soon began using a more colorful — and more descriptive — term: the "fish scale." Looking at this small, wafer-thin coin as its silvery surface glistened in the sun, it looked for all the world like a scale on a newly caught fish.

The silver and nickel three-cent pieces were minted side by side from 1865 until 1873, when the trime was discontinued. The nickel version lingered until 1889.

The five-cent nickel also had a silver antecedent. The original Mint Act of 1792 had provided for the issuance of a coin with a face value of five cents, but that coin was made primarily of silver and was called the "half dime." And that's exactly what it was – a coin half the size of the dime and of the same composition.

The half dime and nickel five-cent piece co-existed at the Mint for eight years, but the silver coin was dumped after its final production run in 1873. The nickel, of course, remains a current coin to this day.

Morgan Silver Dollar

Old-time silver dollars have long been referred to as "cartwheels" because their hefty size reminded many Americans of the wooden wheels on their wagons. The most widely collected cart-

Morgan Silver Dollar

wheel is the Morgan silver dollar, named for the man who designed it, Mint engraver George T. Morgan.

The coin's generic name is "Liberty Head dollar," because it features a quaint, old-fashioned portrait of Miss Liberty. But in some parts of the country, especially the South, people took to calling it the "bow-tie dollar" because from their perspective, the ribbon near the base of its reverse resembled a bow tie.

Saint-Gaudens Double Eagle

The Morgan dollar is among several coins referred to by the names of their designers. Perhaps the most prestigious – and most beautiful – is the magnificent Saint-Gaudens Double Eagle, which many consider to be the loveliest coin ever minted by Uncle Sam. The coin's designer, Augustus Saint-Gaudens, was America's pre-eminent sculptor at the turn of the 20th century.

Saint-Gaudens
Double Eagle

Although the term "Saint" is simply short for "Saint-Gaudens," it also serves, however unintentionally, as an apt epithet summing up the virtue of this exquisite gold piece. In a way, it makes this particular "rose" even more fragrant.

Multiple names also have been used through the years to denote the grade of the very same coin. The adjectival term "gem uncirculated" is generally applied to a coin that is graded Mint State-64 to Mint State-66 by a certification service.

And, while you're at it, be sure to keep up with any new names or numbers that might come into usage as time goes by. History has shown that in the coin market, new varieties of "roses" are being developed just about all the time. Like plus grades being used by leading grading services.

Liberty Head Nickel

The half dollar, quarter and dime designed by Mint engraver Charles E. Barber are commonly lumped together as "Barber coins." Their more official name, though, is "Liberty Head coins." But both terms work equally well.

Liberty Head Nickel

Barber also designed the Liberty Head nickel, but his name isn't as closely associated with that coin's nomenclature – perhaps because it was released independently of the others, in a different metal and with a different design. Its more common alternative name is "V nickel," because it bears the large letter "V" (the Roman numeral for 5) on its reverse.

The Many Names of Paper Money

$10 Bill

Paper money also has given rise to a variety of interesting colloquial names. "Deuce" (for the $2 bill), "5-spot" (for the $5) and "10-spot" (for the $10) are used for obvious reasons. "C-note" (for the $100) reflects the fact that "C" is the Roman numeral for 100, and also might be considered shorthand for "century note." Another common nickname for $100 bills is "Benjamins" – a reference to Benjamin Franklin, the man whose portrait they bear.

"Fin" and "sawbuck" are terms whose derivation takes a little more explanation. "Fin" – a slang name for the $5 bill – traces its origin to "finf," the Yiddish word for "five." And that, in turn, comes from the Old High German word "funf."

"Sawbuck" became an unofficial name for the $10 bill because of a visual coincidence. The large letter "X" (the Roman numeral for 10) on early U.S. $10 bills reminded many Americans of the sawhorse, a contraption with X-shaped supports at each end used to hold wood for cutting.

The term "buck" as a synonym for "dollar" is said to date from the 18th century, when deerskin was a common medium of exchange between American Indians and European settlers. A male deer, of course, is a buck and traders began to use "buck" virtually as a unit of value – a practice that continued even after deerskin receded in importance as a form of quasi-currency.

The expression "passing the buck" is a variation on the same theme, but it has more to do with antes than with antlers. It goes back to the Wild West in the late 19th century, when poker players used a marker called "the buck" to designate the dealer in each game. This "buck" was commonly a knife with a handle made of buckhorn. When a new player took over as dealer, the buck was passed.

"A grand" didn't refer to the $1,000 bill when people started using that expression in the early 1900s – even though $1,000 bills (no longer printed today) were available at the time. It was short for an unspecified "grand sum" of money. Before long, however, common usage rounded off that figure to $1,000 – a grand sum indeed at a time when many Americans were toiling 12 hours a day, six days a week, for paychecks of $12.50 or less.

The French Origins of the Dixies and Dimes

Prior to the introduction of U.S. paper money in 1862, currency was issued privately by state-chartered banks. In Louisiana, which had – and still has – strong French influence, banks issued $10 bills with the word "Dix," French for "10," on the reverse. English-speaking Southerners took to calling these notes "Dixies," and Cajun-speaking parts of Louisiana came to be known as "Dixieland."

In time, the term "Dixie" gained wider usage and evolved into a synonym for the Southern states as a whole. Thus, an entire region might well have derived its name from a piece of paper money.

The word "dime" also can be traced back to France. "Disme" means "one-tenth" in French, and this was the name chosen for the coin worth one-tenth of a dollar in the U.S. coinage system established in 1792. The term was later Americanized to "dime," although the pronunciation remained the same.

The word "disme" never appeared on a regular-issue U.S. coin, but did make a cameo appearance on a handful of provisional 10-cent pieces dated 1792 – four years before the start of regular dime production. Similarly, the words "half disme" can be found on a small number of 1792 five-cent pieces made before the Mint's official opening.

The Lincoln Penny: 100 Years, Many Names

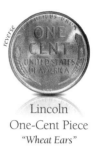 

Lincoln
One-Cent Piece
"Wheat Ears"

Lincoln
One-Cent Piece
"Memorial"

Not surprisingly, the Lincoln cent – the longest-running coin in U.S. history – has spawned numerous nick-names. Put another way, it has been fertile ground for numismatic "roses" with other names.

Lincoln cents from the first 50 years, from 1909 through 1958, are widely referred to as "wheaties" because of the symmetrical ears of wheat depicted along the side borders of the reverse. Those from 1959 through 2008 are called "Memorial cents" because the Lincoln Memorial is shown on the reverse.

The zinc-coated steel cents issued on a wartime emergency basis in 1943 are variously described as "steelies" or "white cents" – the latter because their shiny gray color made them look like dimes when they were new.

Just recently, shorthand names have been coined for the four special cents dated 2009, which commemorate the 200th anniversary of Abraham Lincoln's birth (and the 100th anniversary of the Lincoln cent) by portraying four distinct phases of his life.

The four coins have been dubbed the "Birthplace," "Formative Years," "Professional Life" and "Presidency" cents. In order, they spotlight Lincoln's birth in a log cabin and early boyhood in Kentucky; his growth to manhood in Indiana; his career as a lawyer and legislator in Illinois; and his time as president in Washington, D.C.

A Colorful Bouquet of American Coin Names

Some of the words and phrases used by Americans to describe their coins and currency have been garden-variety terms – predictable and even a little drab. Others have been vivid and compelling. Either way, those pieces of money – like the Shakespearean rose – have always been esteemed because of what they are, not what they're called.

What's in their names? A colorful bouquet of American beauties.

The following terms appear throughout this book. For the sake of the collector who is not familiar with them, these terms are defined in this section.

Abrasion: A mark on a coin caused by contact with another coin.

Bagmark: A mark on a coin caused by contact with other coins when placed inside a bag for shipment to a bank. Most Indian gold coins, as do many United States gold coins, show extensive bagmarks from this process.

Bela Lyon Pratt: The Boston-based artist who was responsible for the original design of the Indian Head Quarter Eagle and Half Eagle.

Border: A design element employing a raised circle with the outer circumference called the rim. On the Indian Head Quarter and Half Eagle, there is no border. There is a border on the Indian Eagles.

Business Strike: A coin, which was struck for general circulation. Business strikes were intended to be used in the normal course of commerce. Also known as a "circulation strike."

Clashmarks: Impressions of a portion of the detail of one side of a coin onto another in the field of a die facing it. Clashmarks occur when dies strike each other during the coinage process without a planchet or blank between them.

Comparative Rarity: The relative rarity of a specific coin in a specific grade when compared to another coin of the same type in the same grade.

Condition Census: A ranking of the five or six finest known examples of a specific issue and ties.

Copper Spots: Gold coins contain 90% gold and 10% copper. During the alloying process, some of the copper can rise to the surface and appear as "spots." In the past, these spots were ignored (and even appreciated) by collectors. Today, they are considered detracting only if they are large and placed in very obvious spots or exist in very large quantities. They are not considered as much of a detraction as damage (bagmarks) or lack of detail (weak strike). For a good example see the 1930-S $10 Indian pictured on page 230.

Die: A piece of fabricated steel, which stamps the design into a planchet.

Die Variety: Distinct varieties within a specific issue caused by using and/or combining new dies within a coinage run. There are very few die varieties in the Indian Head Quarter Eagle series, Half Eagle and Eagle series.

E Pluribus Unum: Motto on United States coinage meaning many uniting into one. Roughly translated "Out of Many, One."

Edge: The cylindrical boundary of a coin.

Edge Reeding: Raised ribs on the edge of a coin, which serve as an anti-counterfeiting and anti-shaving device. All Indian Head Quarter and Half Eagles have a reeded edge.

Edge Stars: The edge of the $10 Indian initially had 46 stars to signify the states of the union instead of having a reeded edge like its predecessor. In 1912 the number of stars was increased to 48.

Eye Appeal: A combination of characteristics such as luster, strike and coloration, which make a coin, literally, "appealing to the eye."

Grade: The rating of a coin's place on a numerical scale, which encompasses the range between extreme wear and perfection.

Hairlines: Fine scratches, which are caused by cleaning a coin with an abrasive.

High Grade Rarity: Determined by the total number of coins that exist in MS65 grades and higher.

Hoard: A group of coins, which can vary greatly in size, which have been taken off the market by a non-numismatic source and, which re-enter the market through a numismatic source. A hoard may contain one specific date or many dates. When a hoard contains multiple examples of one date, this issue may lose value, but other dates, which share its design may gain value through increased collector demand.

Incuse Design: When the major design elements of a coin appear in relief that is lower than the surrounding fields. The only two American coins with an incuse design are the Indian Head Quarter Eagle and Half Eagle.

Key Date: A date in a series, which is recognized as an especially difficult date to locate in all grades.

Matte Proof: A variant type of proof coin that originated in Europe, but was used on American coinage from 1908 through 1916 (and on rare occasions in the 1920's and the 1930's). On such coins, the surfaces have a dull, sandblast finish as opposed to the reflectiveness seen on Brilliant Proofs.

Mintmark: A letter or symbol that identifies the mint that produced a coin. As an example, the letter "S" indicates that a United States coin was struck at the San Francisco Mint. Located near the reverse edge at seven o'clock left of arrow tips on Indian Quarter Eagles, Indian Half Eagles and Indian Eagles.

Mint State: A coin with no wear. Mint State coins are rated on a scale, which goes from Mint State-60 to Mint State-70.

NGC: Numismatic Guaranty Corporation, an East Coast third party grader and authenticator of coins.

Obverse: The front or the "head" side of a coin. Usually the side bearing a face is considered the obverse and gives the coin its name, as in the "Indian Head" Quarter Eagle. In some instances, such as the 'Buffalo' nickel, the reverse image proves so popular that the coin becomes known by its name.

Overall Rarity: A term, which refers to the total number of examples known of a specific issue. PCGS: The Professional Coin Grading Service, a West Coast third party grader and authenticator of coins.

PCGS Secure Plus Holdered Coins: These coins are laser scanned for digital images that are entered into the PCGS' database, which ensures that the coin will be identified if it ever makes a return trip back to PCGS. This ensures greater consistency with grading, enhances counterfeit and alteration detection and increases the likelihood of recovery if a coin is ever stolen. These holders have a unique shield icon as part of the holder's insert.

Pedigree: The chain of ownership of a coin or a collection. A coin pedigreed to a famous collection typically carries a small premium over a non-pedigreed coin.

Planchet: The blank metal disk upon which a coin is stamped.

Population Report: A listing published by both NGC and PCGS, which lists the number of coins graded and how the individual coins break down. A coin with a known population of three specimens may be said to be a "Pop 3" coin.

Proof: A coin, which is struck specially for collectors on a specially prepared planchet. Proof coins receive multiple blows of the dies and afforded special care and handling. Indian head gold coins were made in both Roman and matte proof finishes.

Provenance: See "Pedigree."

Reverse: The back or the "tail" side of a coin.

Roman Finish Proof: This brilliant, but not mirror-like finish, was typically used for gold coin proofs struck in 1909 and 1910. It is also referred to as a satin finish by some.

Saint-Gaudens, Augustus: Considered by many the greatest of modern sculptors. At the bequest of Theodore Roosevelt, he designed new $10 and $20 Gold coins released in 1907.

Set Premium: Sometimes, a complete set of coins that has been assembled in conjunction with an expert professional numismatist is worth more than the sum of the individual pieces it contains. This is known as a "set premium" by numismatists.

Sleeper: A coin, which is underrated and undervalued is said to be a "sleeper."

"Weak Mintmark" Designation: On certain Indian Head Quarter Eagles, most notably the 1911-D, the mintmark is so weakly struck that it is very difficult to see with the naked eye. Both PCGS and NGC designate coins with very faint mintmarks as "Weak Mintmark" and these are accorded reduced values by collectors.

Weak Strike: A coin, which shows inferior detail as a result of the striking process. A weakly struck coin is only accorded a reduced value if most examples of the specific date in question are well struck. An example is the 1911 "Weak D."

Well Struck: A coin, which shows good detail as the result of the striking process. A well struck coin is accorded high value if most examples of the specific date in question are weakly struck.

Uncirculated: A coin with no wear. See "Mint State."

Bibliography

ArtCyclopedia. Website. "Augustus Saint-Gaudens." http://www.artcyclopedia.com/artists/saint-gaudens_augustus.html: ArtCyclopedia, 7/11/2006.

AskArt. Website. "Bela Lyon Pratt (1867 - 1917)." Bela Pratt - Artist, Art - Bela Lyon Pratt. http://www.askart.com/askart/artist.aspx?artist=10319:2/6/2006.

Brainy History. Website. "19067 in History." http://www.brainyhistory.com/years/1907.html: BrainyMedia.com, 6/5/2006.

Breen, Walter, Book. Complete Encyclopedia of U.S. and Colonial Coins. New York: Doubleday, 1988.

Castleman, Michael. Website. "Grace Under Fire." http://www.smithsonianmagazine.com/issues/2006/april/earthquake.php?page=1: Smithsonian Institution, 7/17/2006.

CoinFacts.com. Website. "1787 Massachusetts Half Cent." http://www.coinfacts.com/colonial_coins/massachusetts_coppers/1787_ma_half_cents/1787_ma_half_cent_ryder_04_C.htm: Collectors Universe, 3/13/2006.

_CoinFacts, "1854 Gold Dollar - Indian Head." http://www.coinfacts.com/gold_dollars/1854_gold_dollar_type2.htm: Collectors Universe, 3/13/2006.

_CoinFacts, "1908 $5 or Half Eagle." http://www.coinfacts.com/half_eaglesindian_head_half_eagles/1908_indian_head_half_eagle. htm: Collectors Universe, 3/13/2006.

_CoinFacts, "Massachusetts Copper Coins (1787-1788)." http://www.coinfacts.com/colonial_coins/massachusetts_coppers/ma_copper_coins.htm: Collectors Universe, 3/13/2006.

_CoinFacts, "The History of the Sacagewea Dollar." http://www.coinfacts.com/historical_notes/history_of_the_sacagawea_dollar.htm: Collectors Universe, 3/13/2006.

Coin-n-Medal Collectors' Asylum. Website. "The Quarter Eagles of Bela Lyon Pratt." The Quarter Eagles of Bela Lyon Pratt. http://www.coins-n-medals.com/Exhibits/pratt/pratt.html:2/6/2006.

CoinResource. Website. "Indian Head Quarter Eagles 1908-1929 Coin Guide." http://www.coinresource.com/guide/photograde/pg_$2IndianHeadQuarterEagle.htm: CoinResource, 2/8/2006.
Columbia University Press. Website. "Saint-Gaudens, Augustus." http://www.answers.com/main/ntquery?method=4&dsid=2222&dekey=Augustus+Saint-Gaudens&curtab=2222_1&linktext=Augustus%20Saint-Gaudens: Answers.com, 3/13/2006.

Deisher, Beth et al, Book. Coin World Almanac. Sidney, Ohio: Amos Press, 2000.

Dictionary.com. Website. "Intaglio." http://dictionary.reference.com/search?q=intaglio: Dictionary.com, 3/14/2006.

eBay (rivershack1). Website. Running Antelope 1977. http://cgi.ebay.com/
RUNNING-ANTELOPE-1977-AMERICAN-NUMISMATIC-
ASSOC_W0QQitemZ8370734602QQcategoryZ376QQcmdZViewItemebayphotohosting:2/6/2006.

Fitzgerald, Dr. Thomas. Website. "The Circulating Coin Designs Of The 20th Century." http://www.nasc.net
Articles/circulating_coin_designs.htm: The Numismatic Association of Southern California, 2/8/2006.

_Fitzgerald, Dr. Thomas. Website. "Through the Numismatic Glass: Who Was Henry Hering?."
http://www.coinmall.com/CSNA/art019.htm: California State Numismatic Association, 6/2/2006.

_Fitzgerald, The Circulating Coin Designs of the 20th Century.
http://www.nasc.net/Articles/circulating_coin_designs.htm: The Numismatic Association of Southern California, 7/11/2006.

Fontenot, Dale. Website. "An Utterly Unique Gold Coin." US Gold - $2 _ Indian. http://www.intcurrency.com
results.cfm?catID=49&subcatID=72:2/6/2006.

Fuljenz, Mike, Book Series. A Collector's Guide to Indian Head Quarter Eagles. A Collector's Guide. Beaumont, TX

Gable, John Allen. Website. "Introduction." Theodore Roosevelt Cyclopedia.
http://www.theodoreroosevelt.org/TR%20Web%20Book/TR_CD_to_HTML16.html: Theodore Roosevelt
Association and Meckler, 7/14/2006.

Garrett, Jeff and Ron Guth, Book. Encyclopedia of U.S. Gold Coins 1795-1933. Atlanta, Georgia: Whitman
Publishing, 2006

Giedroyc, Richard. Website. "The History of the United States $10 Gold Piece." http://www.coinfacts.com/
historical_notes/history_of_the_eagle.htm: Coinfacts.com, 6/2/2006.

Hart, Bushnell Albert and William Allen White. Website. "The Theodore Roosevelt Cyclopedia: Introduction."
http://www.theodoreroosevelt.org/TR%20Web%20Book/Index.html:3/13/2006.

IMDb. Website. "Chief Thundercloud." http://www.imdb.com/name/nm0862086/:2/8/2006.

Infoplease. Website. "1908." http://www.infoplease.com/year/1908.html: Infoplease.com, 5/12/2006.

InformationPlease. Website. "Theodore Roosevelt." http://www.infoplease.com/ipa/A0760610.html:
Pearson Education, 4/7/2006.

Johnson, Dick. Website. "The Importance of Relief on Coins and Medals."
http://www.coinbooks.org/club_nbs_esylum_v06n54.html: E-Sylum, 12/21/2003.

Leach, Frank. Book. "Official Life in Washington, from "Recollections of a Newspaperman - A Record of Life and
Events in California"." http://www.coinfacts.com/historical_notes/frank_leach.htm: Coinfacts.com, 7/17/2006.

_Leach, Frank, Book. RECOLLECTIONS OF A NEWSPAPER MAN A Record of Life and Events in California.
San Francisco: Samual Levinson, 1917.

_Leach, Frank. Website. "Great Earthquake and Fire of 1906."
http://www.sfmuseum.org/1906.2/ew22.html: Virtual Museum of San Francisco, 5/12/2006.

Leonard, Eric. Website. "United States Coins of the 20th Century." 20th Century U.S. Coins. http://www.rrcoins.net/20th_Century_Coins.htm: Crescent City Coin Club, 2/8/2006.

LoveToKnow Corp.. Website. "Rare Early Coins of the United States Mint." http://www.2020site.org/coins/quartereagle.html: LoveToKnow Corp., 3/1/3/2006.

_LoveToKnow, "Immunis Columbia - 1787." http://www.2020site.org/coins/immuniscolumbia.html: LoveToKnow Corp., 3/13/2006.

Massachusetts Historical Society, The. Website. "Who Was William Sturgis Bigelow?." http://www.masshist.org/cabinet/may2002/bigelow.htm: The Massachusetts Historical Society, 3/13/2006.

Moran, Mike. "Augustus Saint-Gaudens: American Michelangelo." The Numismatist (Colorado Springs, CO), September 2003, 33-37.

Moran, Mike. "Earthquake!." Numismatist (Colorado Springs, CO), April 2006, 36-48.

Morris County Library. Website. "How Much Did It Cost in Morris County, New Jersey?." http://www.gti.net/mocolib1/prices/1906.html: Morris County Library, 6/7/2006.

Mudd, Douglas. Email. "What Is "Incuse," Really?." Douglas Mudd, Curator of Exhibitions, American Numismatic Association. 4/11/2006.

Museum Gazette, The. Website. "Charles E. Barber, Artist in Metal." http://www.nps.gov/jeff/Gazettes/CBarber.htm: Jefferson National Expansion Memorial, 5/12/2006.

National Gallery of Art, the collection. Website. "Bela Lyon Pratt." Bela Lyon Pratt. http://www.nga.gov/cgi-bin/pbio?551644:2/6/2006.

NativeAmericans.com. Website. "Sioux Tribe." Native Americans - Sioux. http://www.nativeamericans.com/Sioux.htm:2/6/2006.

New York Times. Website. "Chief Thundercloud." http://movies2.nytimes.com/gst/movies/filmography.html?p_id=12814: New York Times, 2/8/1006.

Numismatic Guaranty Corporation. Website. "1908-29 HALF EAGLE INDIAN HEAD." http://www.collectorusa.com/library.php?page=other&id=99: Collector USA, 2/8/2006.

ParkNet, National Park Service. Website. "Who Was Augustus Saint-Gaudens?." http://www.cr.nps.gov/nr/twhp/wwwlps/lessons/48GAUDENS/48facts1.htm: ParkNet, National Park Service, 7/12/2006.

PBS. Website. "Augustus Saint-Gaudens." http://www.pbs.org/wnet/americanmasters/database/saint-gaudens_a.html: Public Broadcasting System, 3/13/2006.

Pike County Historical Society, The. Website. "Chief Thundercloud." http://www.pikehistory.org/thunderc.htm:2/8/2006.

Prout, Curtis. Website. "Vita: William Stugis Bigelow." http://128.103.142.209/issues/so97/vita.html: Harvard Magazine, 3/13/2006.

Bibliography

Rare Coin Museum. Website. "$10 Indian Head Gold." http://rarecoins.org/
10_indian_gold.htm: Rare Coin Museum, 6/2/2006.

Reiter, Ed. Website. "Bela Lyon Pratt: Overlooked Designed of Two Underrated Coins." Same.
http://www.pcgs.com/articles/article1612.chtml: Professional Coin Grading Service (PCGS), 2/6/2006.

Roach, Steven. Website. "A History and Intepretation of Bela Lyon Pratt's Indian Designs."
http://www.pcgs.com/articles/article1826.chtml: Professional Coin Grading Service, 2/8/2006.

   _Roach, "The Path Of America's Indian: Changes In The Depiction Of The American Indian On Regular Issue
American Coinage from Longacre To Fraser." http://www.pcgs.com/articles/article1388.chtml: Professional
Coin Grading Service, 5/10/2006.

Robinson, B.A.. Website. "The U.S. National Mottos: Their History & Constitutionality."
http://www.religioustolerance.org/nat_mott.htm: Ontario Consultants on Religious Tolerance, 6/6/2006.

Roosevelt, Franklin D.. Website. "Executive Order 6102 - Requiring Gold Coin, Gold Bullion,
and Gold Certificates to be Delivered to the Government." The American Presidency Project. http://www.presi-
dency.ucsb.edu/ws/index.php?pid=14611&st=&st1=: Americanpresidency.org, John Woolley
and Gerhard Peters, 6/7/2006.

Saint-Gaudens National Historic Site. Website. "Annie Page and Alice Butler." http://www.sgnhs.org/Augus-
tus%20SGaudens%20CD-HTML/Models/ButlerAndPage.htm: Saint-Gaudens National Historic Site, 7/13/2006.

   _Saint-Gaudens National Historic Site. Website. "One Cent Piece, 1905-6."
http://www.sgnhs.org/Augustus%20SGaudens%20CD-HTML/CoinsAndMedals/OneCent.htm:
Saint-Gaudens National Historic Site, 7/13/2006.

   _Saint-Gaudens National Historic Site. Website. "Augustus Saint-Gaudens, 1908, by Kenyon Cox."
http://www.sgnhs.org/Augustus%20SGaudens%20CD-HTML/Portraits/Cox.htm: Saint-Gaudens National
Historic Site, 7/14/2006.

   _Saint-Gaudens National Historic Site. Website. "A Life in Art: An American Master."
http://www.sgnhs.org/gusart.html: Saint-Gaudens National Historic Site, 7/14/2006.

   _Saint-Gaudens National Historical Site. Website. "A Life in Art: An American Master."
http://www.sgnhs.org/gusart.html: Saint-Gaudens National Historical Site, 3/13/2006.

Sculptor.org. Website. Sculptor.Org - Bela Lyon Pratt (1867-1917).
http://www.sculptor.org/Sculptors/ByName/BelaLyonPratt.htm: Sculptor.org, 2/6/2006.

Senechal, Roberta. Website. The Springfield Race Riot of 1908. http://www.lib.niu.edu/ipo/1996/iht329622.html:
Illinois Periodicals Online, Northern Illinois University Libraries, 2/8/2006.

Smithsonian Institution. Website. "Chief Thundercloud (1856-1916)." http://www.si.edu/harcourt/npg/col/
native/thunder.htm: Smithsonian Institution, 2/8/2006.

   _Smithsonian Institution, "Theodore Roosevelt: Icon of the Century - Introduction."
http://www.npg.si.edu/exh/roosevelt/trintro2.htm: Smithsonian Institution, 2/7/2006.

Smithsonian National Museum of American History. Website. "Roosevelt Inaugural Medal, 1905." Legendary Coins & Currency. http://americanhistory.si.edu/coins/printable/coin.cfm?coincode=2_01&coinside=front: Smithsonian National Museum of American History, 7/12/2006.

Snow Owl. Website. "Running Antelope." Native Leaders Past & Presentation. http://www.snowwowl.com/nativeleaders/runningantelope.html: Snow Owl, 5/11/2006.

The Museum Gazette. Website. "Charles Barber, Artist in Metal." http://www.nps.gov/jeff/Gazettes/CBarber.htm: Jefferson National Expansion Memorial, 7/14/2006.

Theodore Roosevelt Association. Website. "A Photographic Look at the Life of Theodore Roosevelt." http://www.theodoreroosevelt.org/life/biopictures.htm: Theodore Roosevelt Association, 7/13/2006.

United States Department of the Treasury. Website. "History of "In God We Trust"." Fact Sheets: Currency & Coins. http://www.treasury.gov/education/fact-sheets/currency/in-god-we-trust.shtml: United States Department of the Treasury, 6/6/2006.

United States Mint. Website. "Directors of the U.S. Mint - 1792-Present." http://www.usmint.gov/about_the_mint/index.cfm?flash=yes&action=Past_directors: United States Mint, U.S. Dept. of Treasury, 7/17/2006.

_United States Mint, "American Eagle Gold Bullion Coins." http://www.usmint.gov/mint_programs/american_eagles/index.cfm?Action=american_eagle_gold: United States Mint, 3/13/2006.

_United States Mint, "American Eagle Silver Bullion Coins." http://www.usmint.gov/mint_programs/american_eagles/index.cfm?Action=american_eagle_silver: United States Mint, 3/13/2006.

_United States Mint, "American Eagle Platinum Bullion Coins." http://www.usmint.gov/mint_programs/american_eagles/index.cfm?Action=american_eagle_platinum: United States Mint, 3/13/2006.

US Treasury. Website. "Indian Head Cent." http://www.ustreas.gov/education/fact-sheets/currency/indian-head.shtml: United States Department of the Treasury, 3/13/2006.

What-a-Character.com. Website. "Chief Thundercloud." http://www.what-a-character.com/cgi-bin/display.cgi?id=ThundercloudC:2/8/2006.

White House, The. Website. "Theodore Roosevelt." Biography of Theodore Roosevelt. http://www.whitehouse.gov/history/presidents/tr26.html: Whitehouse.gov, 4/7/2006.

Whitehouse, David. Website. "Mystery Space Blast "Solved"." Mystery Space Blast "Solved". http://news.bbc.co.uk/1/hi/sci/tech/1628806.stm: BBC News, 2/6/2006.

Wikipedia. Website. "1907." http://en.wikipedia.org/wiki/1907: Wikipedia, 6/5/2006.

_Wikipedia, "1908." http://en.wikipedia.org/wiki/1908:2/8/2006.

_Wikipedia, "Augustus Saint-Gaudens." http://en.wikipedia.org/wiki/Augustus_Saint-Gaudens: Wikipedia, 3/13/2006.

_Wikipedia. Website. "Bela Pratt." Bela Pratt. http://en.wikipedia.org/wiki/Bela_Lyon_Pratt:2/6/2006.

Bibliography

_Wikepedia. Website. "Boston Brahmin."   http://www.answers.com/main/ntquery?s=Boston%20Brahmin&gwp=16: Answers.com,   3/13/2006.

_Wikipedia. Website. "Charles E. Barber." http://en.wikipedia.org/wiki/Charles_E._Barber: Wikipedia, 7/14/2006.

_Wikipedia. Website. "eagle." eagle. http://www.answers.com/main/ntquery;jsessionid=an52ikrqpb0ae?method=4&dsid=2222&dekey=Eagle+%28U.S.+coin%29&gwp=8&curtab=2222_1&sbid=lc04a&linktext=eagles: Answers.com, 2/6/2006.

_Wikipedia. Website. "In God We Trust." http://en.wikipedia.org/wiki/In_God_We_Trust: Wikipedia, 6/6/2006.

_Wikipedia. Website. "Leon Czolgosz." http://en.wikipedia.org/wiki/Leon_Czolgosz: Wikipedia, 7/11/2006.

_Wikipedia, "Quarter Eagle." http://en.wikipedia.org/wiki/Quarter_eagle:2/8/2006.

_Wikipedia. Website. "Theodore Roosevelt." http://en.wikipedia.org/wiki/Theodore_Roosevelt: Wikipedia, 7/13/2006.

_Wikipedia, "United States Coinage." Same. http://www.absoluteastronomy.com/reference/united_states_coinage:2/7/2006.

_Wikipedia, "William Barber." http://en.wikipedia.org/wiki/William_Barber: Wikipedia, 5/12/2006.

_Wikipedia. Website. "William McKinley." http://en.wikipedia.org/wiki/William_McKinley: Wikipedia, 7/11/2006.

Yeoman, R.S., Book, Edition. The Official Red Book - A Guide Book of United States Coins 2006. Bressett, Kenneth. 59th Edition. Atlanta, GA: Whitman Publishing LLC, 2005.

INDEX